THE ART OF
PRESERVING

By Jacqueline Wejman
Essays by Charles St. Peter

Drawings by Holly Zapp

101 Productions
San Francisco

Distributed to the book trade in the United States
by Charles Scribner's Sons, New York.

Published by 101 Productions
834 Mission Street
San Francisco, California 94103

Library of Congress Cataloging in Publication Data

Wejman, Jacqueline, 1925–
    The art of preserving.

    Enl. ed. of: Jams & jellies. 1975.
    Bibliography: p.
    Includes index.
    1. Jam.   2. Jelly.   I. St. Peter, Charles, 1917–
II. Title.
TX612.J3W44   1983   641.8'52   83-6303
ISBN 0-89286-212-2

Contents

TO GENEVIEVE AND JOHN WITHOUT WHOM . . .

Introduction

Every suburban and country household should plant and nurture a garden and raise small fruits; then during the summer from the products of his effort the bulk of the food for the family be provided and all surplus should be carefully preserved for future use. The economic conditions of the age demand this.

Janet M. Hill, August 1, 1915
Canning, Preserving and Jelly Making

In writing this book we have hoped to inspire the creative cook to preserve the munificence of the bush and orchard for the family and as gifts for friends. There is a trend today among our younger people to turn back to the land for organic foods and to preserve garden produce, some of which they grow themselves. There is a revival of the old-fashioned ways of buying fruits in quantity when they are most reasonable in price, and "putting them by" against higher prices which have climbed so inexorably in these inflationary times.

Well-filled shelves of jams and jellies are a deep satisfaction as well as a source of tempting desserts and tea table treats for unexpected guests. In making our own jams and jellies, we combine economy and flavor in the tradition of our grandmothers, and reject the artificial colorings, flavorings and preservatives of the commercial product.

I Basics of Preserving

In the Beginning

T HE ART of preserving jams and jellies was perfected as recently as the 18th or early 19th centuries, unlike other preserving methods such as freezing, salting, curing, drying and pickling which have been with us since cave-dwelling days. Who fathered the process of preserving food through the use of heat is a matter of mild dispute, but most source books credit Nicolas Appert, a Parisian confectioner and distiller. He was a man born in modest circumstances, who worked and experimented with foods all his life. His work intensified when the French government in 1795 announced a prize of 12,000 francs for the discovery of a way of preserving food so that it could be transported to the armies of the Revolution over great distances without spoiling. "But the great advantage of this method consists principally in its application to the service of the Navy," Appert wrote. "It will supply fresh and wholesome provisions for his Majesty's vessels on long voyages with a saving of more than fifty per cent."

With scarce funds and limited equipment, Appert ploddingly pursued the golden carrot which the government had dangled before him. There followed a series of small successes, and year after year he drew closer to the secret and, finally, *voilà!* In 1810, he took out a patent on his process, and the Board of Arts and Manufacturers of the Ministry of the Interior awarded him the 12,000 francs. In the same year he published a book, *The Art of Preserving All Kinds of Animal and Vegetable Substances for Several Years.*

The book details the process. Methods used today are simply refinements of the Appert patent. The modern houseperson can dispense with most of the implements through which Appert perfected the art: a three-legged bottle-boot and a batt for corking; a five-legged stool for tieing on the cork; or a machine for twisting and cutting to proper length the iron wire for binding the corks. Today mason jars, with their metal domes which seal in the process of heating, make jam and jelly preserving a simple matter.

The 12,000 franc prize was used to found the House of Appert, and to begin canning and preserving foods on a commercial basis. Appert was now 62 years of age. An etching by M. Blanchard shows him as a man of sculpted features, tall of brow and scant of hair. The success of his preserving method depended on the exclusion of air, although Appert arrived at his conclusion by direct observation rather than by scientific theory. It was Louis Pasteur who provided the correct explanation: fermentation and decay of food was caused by microorganisms, such as bacteria, moulds and yeast present in the food, water and air. Pasteur's experiments with wine, vinegar and milk wedded his name to the process, pasteurization.

Actually, his method was merely a reprise of the process developed by the industrious and self-effacing Appert. Pasteur wrote in 1873, "When I published the first result of my experimentation on the possible preservation and conservation of wine by preliminary heating, it was evident I only made a new application of the method of Appert, but I was absolutely ignorant that Appert had devised this same application a long time before me."

On the other side of the Channel, doubts were cast upon Appert's distinction as the first to preserve food by heat. An article in the *Edinburgh Review* of 1814 observed that in 1808 an Englishman, Thomas Saddington, had received an award from the Society of Arts for a paper on *A New Method of Preserving Various Sorts of English Garden and Orchard Fruits, without Sugar.* The article adds that in 1810, the same year in which Appert had received his patent and published his book, another Englishman, Peter Durand, received a patent on an invention "communicated to him by a certain foreigner residing abroad," on the *Method of Preserving Animal Food, Vegetable Food and other Perishable Articles for a Long Time from Perishing or Becoming Useless.*

The staunchest defender of Appert's claim is Kate Golden Bitting, the esteemed American bibliographer of cookery, whose collection reposes in the Library of Congress. Her strongest case is made in a foreword to *Appertising,* a book on commercial canning. The "certain foreigner residing abroad" was none other than Appert, she insists. As early as 1804, a letter to the maritime prefect at Brest stated that provisions supplied by Appert, which had been lying in a vessel in the roads for three months, remained in good condition. And on March 7, 1807, Rear Admiral Allemand, on board the Imperial Ship le Majesteux, wrote to Appert, ". . . the Captains . . . under my orders . . . tasted the day before yesterday the vegetables I purchased from you fourteen months ago, one bottle of which my maître-d'hôtel had by accident left in the store room. As green peas and beans are just beginning to be gathered, the officers believed your preserved vegetables to be fresh, so well had you succeeded. . . ."

Mrs. Bitting singles out several persons who had hit upon the heat preserving method, but had not followed through, including an anonymous author in 1680. Her bibliography contains a plate from *E. Kidder's Receipts of Pastry and Cookery, etc.,* Edward Kidder, London, 1720, whose method of bottling gooseberries, Damsons, bullace, pears, plums and currants is remarkably close to the Appert method, even to the use of wide-mouthed bottles and corks. She credits the Swedish chemist Schlee with discovering the principle of preserving vinegar, but again it had little effect on practical conservation of foods.

So history gives the nod to Nicolas Appert. So be it. And yet, and yet. . . .

Consider the credentials of Amelia Simmons, author of the first indigenous American cookbook, who signs herself "An American Orphan." In her *American Cookery,* the recipe for preserving Damsons recommends they be put up tight in snuff bottles, stopped up tight so no air nor water can get to them, and that they then be boiled, cooled and stored in a cool place where they will keep 12 months if properly stoppered. Or long enough to provision most Napoleonic campaigns. The book was published in 1796.

EQUIPMENT

- The first necessary piece of equipment is a large eight- to ten-quart *preserving kettle.* The size is of great importance, for it will allow rapid boiling without the contents splashing over the stove as fruit-sugar mixtures expand. Use a kettle with a broad flat bottom made from heavy aluminum which will prevent sticking. Enamel is inclined to chip; tin, iron and copper spoil the color of some fruits and give a metallic flavor, especially when making chutneys.
- A *long-handled wooden spoon* will not transmit heat and enables the jams to be stirred without getting hot splashes on arms and hands. Also necessary is a *long-handled slotted metal spoon* with a flat bowl for skimming.
- For convenience, a *wide-mouthed funnel* saves spills when putting hot fruit into jars, and makes filling much quicker.
- A *ladle* that lifts the hot fruit from the preserving kettle to the funnel is of great help, as a measuring cup becomes too hot to handle.
- A *jelly or deep-fat thermometer* is a reliable guide for testing the jellying point.
- The following items, which are standard in most kitchens, will be needed: standard *1 quart and 1/4, 1/3, 1/2, 3/4 and 1 cup measures; paring and utility knives; measuring spoons; lemon squeezer; spatula; food chopper or meat grinder; grater; potato masher; wire basket;* and *bowls of various sizes. Household scales* come in most handy, as the best results come from careful measuring. An *electric blender or sieve* is necessary for smooth mixtures such as butters.

- A *jelly bag or cloth,* or some sort of bag, is a necessity for getting the fullest amount of juice out of the fruit. A bag hanging from a tripod which can be hooked onto a bowl may be purchased, or a simple fruit squeezer consisting of a nylon bag with a drawstring closing may be used. A wooden ring goes over the closing of the bag so that the fruit may be squeezed down and the juice will drip through to the bowl. Lacking a bag, a yard of unbleached muslin or cheesecloth, washed and scalded, may be spread over a colander. After the fruit is poured into the cloth, gather the cloth in your hands above the fruit and tie a string around the gathers. Hang the bag over the side of the bowl or tie it to the faucet and let the juice drip into a bowl.

JARS AND HOW TO STERILIZE

Carefully examine the tops of the jars to see that there are no nicks, cracks or sharp edges, as defects prevent airtight seals. Mason, Kerr and Ball jars are obtainable at supermarkets and hardware stores. They are excellent and can be reused each year, providing new lids are used each time to ensure a perfect seal.

If paraffin is used for sealing, select jars or glasses with straight sides. Not only will these make an attractive mold for jellies, but it is easier to dig out the paraffin without its getting into the contents of the jar.

To sterilize jars, wash them in hot suds and rinse in scalding water. In a large kettle, put the jars and lids, cover them with hot water and bring the water to a boil. Boil for five minutes and turn off the heat; let the jars and lids stand in the hot

Basics of Preserving

water. Before the jars are ready to be used, invert them on a rack to dry. Jars should be filled while they are hot. If you are lucky enough to have an automatic dishwasher, put the jars in the rinse water cycle. The degree of heat should be 150° or higher.

ALLOWING HEAD ROOM SPACE AND TO FILL

Head room space is the air space between the lids or paraffin and the contents of the jar. This air space creates suction to insure a perfect vacuum. If jars with self-sealing lids are being used, allow 1/4-inch head room space and screw on lids tightly.

SEALING WITH PARAFFIN

To seal open glasses and jelly jars, fill to within 1/2-inch head room, being sure to first wipe the rim and threads of the jars with a hot damp cloth to remove all particles of food, seeds or spices. While contents are hot, cover with a 1/8-inch layer of melted paraffin. When paraffin has set, add another layer of melted paraffin, tilting and rotating the jar to seal completely. Cover with waxed paper to keep dust out. Paraffin, or household wax of this type, may be found in most large grocery stores.

YIELDS OF JAM AND JELLIES

It is difficult to give an exact yield for jam and jelly recipes, for it will always vary a little depending on the juice content of the fruit. Longer cooked jams will yield less than jams using commercial pectin.

HOW TO TEST JELLY

As the syrup thickens, take a clean wooden spoon, place a small amount of jelly in the bowl of the spoon and cool slightly. Then turn the spoon and allow the jelly to drop from the side of it into the kettle. When the jellying point has been reached, two drops will come together and fall as one drop. This is called sheeting. A jelly thermometer may also be used, the jellying point being reached when it reads 220° to 222°.

BLANCHING

Blanching consists of plunging fruits, e.g., peaches, apricots, tomatoes, etc., into boiling water for a short time. The purpose of this is to shrink the fruit and loosen the skin, making peeling easy. Cold dip usually follows blanching; this is the plunging of the fruit into cold running water for five to 10 seconds. A wire basket for holding the fruit works well for the cold dip.

STORING

Store fruit butters, chutneys, conserves, jams, jellies, marmalades and preserves in a cool, dark place. Label them, including the date and year. They are ready to eat and the flavors have mellowed about two weeks after being made. They will keep until next season's fruits are in and the jars may be refilled again.

PROCESSING IN A WATER BATH

The purpose of a hot water bath is to ensure an airtight vacuum. However, the use of paraffin or hot, sterilized mason, Kerr and Ball lids have proven entirely satisfactory to ensure a vacuum on a jar that has been sterilized and filled with boiling hot preserves. If you wish to use a hot water bath for processing preserves with metal lids, any deep pan or kettle may be used, or a canner may be purchased. Put a wire cake rack or a wooden board on the bottom of the kettle. Pour the hot preserves into the hot, sterilized jars, put the lids in place and screw on the rings tightly. Place the hot jars on the rack or board, being careful that the jars do not touch each other or the bottom and sides of the kettle; allow five to six inches of space between the tops of the jars and the top of the kettle. An old dish towel may be stuffed between the jars to prevent them from touching. Pour hot water down the sides of the kettle until the jars are covered by two inches. Do not pour the water directly over the jars. Bring the water to a boil, and boil covered, over high heat, for 10 minutes. Remove the jars from the kettle with tongs and place them on a towel or wooden board. Make sure the jars are not in a draft or they may crack from the sudden change of temperature. Let them stand for about 24 hours and test the seal by removing the ring. If the seal is good, the lid will be depressed. Or, if you tap the lid with a spoon, it should give a clear ringing sound. If the seal is not good and there are signs of leakage, either use the preserves right away or reprocess them. To reprocess, empty the contents into a kettle, reheat, ladle into hot, sterilized jars and process again in a water bath.

WHY PROBLEMS OCCUR

Spoilage
- Too little sugar used
- Not cooked long enough
- Stored in too warm a place

Mildew
- Used cold, wet jars
- Stored in a damp place
- Not sealed properly (must be airtight)

Crystallization
- Too much sugar used
- Allowed the jam to boil before sugar dissolved
- Left uncovered too long

Basics of Preserving

EQUIVALENTS

1 teaspoon = 1/3 tablespoon
1 tablespoon = 3 teaspoons
1/4 cup = 4 tablespoons
1/3 cup = 5-1/3 tablespoons
1/2 pint = 1 cup
1 pint = 2 cups = 1 pound
1 quart = 2 pints = 2 pounds
1 gallon = 4 quarts = 8 pounds

Approximate Number per Pound
Apples: 4 medium
Apricots: 10 medium
Bananas: 3 medium
Cantaloupes: 1 medium = 2 pounds
Cherries: 3 cups, stemmed
Cranberries: 4-1/2 cups
Figs: 8 medium
Gooseberries: 3 cups
Grapes: 2-1/2 cups, stemmed
Kiwi berries: 7 medium
Lemons: 4 medium
Limes: 7 medium
Nectarines: 4 medium
Onions: 3 medium
Oranges: 2 medium
Papayas: 1 medium
Peaches: 4 medium
Pears: 2 medium
Peppers (sweet green): 6 small
Peppers (sweet red): 4 medium
Persimmons: 2 medium
Plums: 14 medium
Strawberries: 3 cups
Tomatoes: 3 medium

John Mason's Jar

PITY THE POOR consumers. When mind boggling prices on the supermarket shelves turn them to home canning and preserving, the supply of glass jars for the purpose dries up. At this writing a Knight Newspaper dispatch relates sales of glass jars have rocketed 2,500 percent at Ball Corporation in a single year, adding "glass canning jars are almost as tough to find as a home mortgage." Ball Corporation reported its stock of glass containers shrunk from 3,500,000 cases in mid-1973 to 200,000 cases in mid-1974. Rival Kerr Glass Manufacturing Company reports sales up 173 percent and a growing shortage of tinplate for lids. Ball and Kerr account for approximately 90 percent of the Mason jars produced. So the thrifty minded who turned to home gardens find their fruits and vegetables uncontained. By the early 1970's home canning had become a lost art, and lost with it were the millions of jars which were staples of grandmother's day. They were reused season to season, then passed on to the succeeding generation. A woman wrote the *Michigan Farmer* in 1958, "We have a dozen one-quart Mason jars which my husband's grandmother gave us filled with fruit on our wedding day. I am still using them. We have been married 58 years."

The mason jar was the invention of John L. Mason of New York City. A farm boy, he grappled with the method of preserving the fruits of the harvest through the winter months. The problem, he knew, was to cast glass threads at the top of the jar so that an airtight metal cap could be screwed down. In November, 1858, Mason took out two patents, the second being for an "Improved Jar" and the legend "Mason's Patent, November 30, 1858" was to be inscribed on glass jars for decades to follow. Mason went into business making caps for the jars, while the jars were bought from glassblowers who made them from Mason's patented molds. Mason went on to register six more patents on his jars, two on closures and one on a baby bottle. Among his other patents were a folding life raft, a soap dish and a brush holder.

In 1885, the five Ball Brothers of Buffalo, New York, were persuaded by some itinerant Belgian glassblowers to build a small glass factory. They found themselves with more capacity than customers. The brothers scouted around for other products, and discovered that Mason's early patents for the screw top had expired. They were soon turning out mason jars. Within a year, a fire destroyed their small factory; they collected a small amount of insurance and cast about for a place to relocate. Glassmaking consumes infernos of heat, and the Balls had heard of a great natural gas belt in the Middle West, where fuel was cheap and plentiful. (The gas belt is long since exhausted.) President Frank C. Ball visited several Middle Western cities seeking new industries.

While making his rounds, he received a telegram from Muncie, Indiana, a town of which he had never heard. He visited it on a free weekend and found it an unprepossessing town with unpaved streets, but noted of the civic leaders, "The men were all courteous, kind and businesslike." The town contributed $5,000 and donated seven acres of land. In 1888, two furnaces supplying nine pots were turning out the Ball mason jar. Ten years later, the semi-automatic glassblowing device, the "F. C. Ball Machine," was introduced and the days of the glassblower, who relied on his lungs and individual hand-held molds, were numbered. None too soon, because they suffered from the intense heat and were prey to respiratory diseases. (In Venice, three years ago, an agent for Murano's, the celebrated glass house, said there were only about 60 hand glassblowers remaining in the environs because these occupational hazards made it an unattractive trade.)

Along came Alexander Kerr. This eclectic gentleman bought the rights to heat-sealing gaskets on a lacquered metal lid from a German, and wedded it to the spring clip, developed by a California inventor, which held the lid during the preserving process. The Kerr lid vented air during the cooking of the preserves, then hardened tightly on the top of the jar after cooking. In the same year, the first fully automatic glass-making machine was developed and production capacity took a quantum leap. Twelve years later, in 1915, Kerr patented a metal screw band to replace the spring clip and this is the type of airtight closure used on almost all mason jars today. The name Kerr is familiar to all home canners, as he founded the Kerr Glass Manufacturing Company, formerly seated in Sand Springs, Oklahoma, and now headquartered in Los Angeles. For reasons known only to themselves, the Kerrs still imprint "mason" on their jars, even though one of their founders developed and patented the seal that superseded the primitive mason lid.

Back to John Mason, the hero of our story. He is no hero to Dr. Julian Harrison Toulouse, an authority on screw-top glass jars and closures. "There is a certain refrain, repeated with variations by collectors and non-collectors alike, that bothers me. 'Mason invented fruit canning!' 'Mason invented the fruit jar.' 'Mason invented the screw cap.' It is these statements that could best be called inventions."

The good doctor even imputes that Mason got his idea from a mold maker whom he asked for advice after commissioning the artisan to make screw caps for a glass jar. Furthermore, the metallic taste left by Mason's zinc caps slowed their acceptance. Dr. Toulouse cites Robert Arthur as three years ahead of Mason. After Mason came Lewis R. Boyd, Albert G. Smalley and George Putnam who all made significant advances over the Mason jar. The doctor credits Boyd with "saving" the Mason jar in the form of a glass, later opal, liner for Mason's zinc cap.

As we said earlier, back to John Mason. He had married, sired eight daughters—including two pairs of twins—and moved to New Brunswick, New Jersey. He joined the Consolidated Fruit Jar Company and in a few years he had assigned his remaining rights to his jars to Consolidated. Early in the 1890's, he moved to Brooklyn. His daughters married and his wife died in 1898. John Mason returned to New York to spend his last years in a tenement on West 168th Street. In 1902, he died as a charity patient in the House of Relief on Hudson Street in lower Manhattan, at age 70.

TYPES OF PRESERVES

PECTIN

Jams and jellies, regardless of how they are made, must have four ingredients in the right proportion: fruit, pectin, sugar and acid. Pectin may be obtained directly from the fruit itself; underripe fruit contains more than fully ripe. There are two kinds of commercial pectin available: Liquid pectin is derived from apple pectin. Powdered pectin is made from either apple or citrus pectin. Both should be used as directed on the label.

FRUIT BUTTER

Fruit which has been pulped and put through a sieve, colander or blender and cooked with sugar and sometimes spices, until it is thick and creamy enough to spread. Butters are useful to use up large quantities of fruit, as they are considerably reduced in their cooking process. The amount of sugar used varies according to taste, but 1/2 to 2/3 cup for each cup of fruit is standard. Fruit butters should be cooked until a small quantity poured on a cold plate shows no edge of liquid.

CHUTNEY

A condiment made with fruit such as mangoes, peaches, tamarinds and raisins; spices like garlic, chilies and cayenne pepper; and acids like vinegar and lemon juice. Chutneys need long simmering to give a smooth, mellow flavor. They should be rich and thick and may be cooked in large quantities. Good with meats and curries.

CONSERVE

Type of jam made of several fruits (fresh or dried) cooked together with sugar and often with nuts, raisins and/or coconut. A conserve, though cooked like a jam, is usually served as a side dish rather than a spread on bread. The nuts have a better texture and flavor if they are added five to 10 minutes before removing from the heat.

JAM

Fruit crushed, pulped, ground or chopped and cooked with sugar until thick. Use well-ripened but sound berries, apricots, peaches, plums, etc. Jams need to be rich in acid and pectin, so commercial pectin may be used, but follow the directions for its addition carefully. Use 3/4 cup of sugar for each cup of fruit. Jam is cooked when a jelly thermometer reads 220° to 222°, or when the mixture sheets from a wooden spoon (two large drops form, come together and fall as one drop). Do not cook it longer; it may spoil the flavor and make it too thick, as it thickens upon cooling. Jams are used as spreads on bread and toast and as fillings for cakes and pastries.

JELLY

Jelly is the sweet obtained by combining the juice of one or more fruits with sugar, and cooking the mixture until it becomes clear and jewel-like. Good jelly quivers, yet holds its shape when cut. It is tender and its flavor is fresh and fruity. The best fruits for making jelly are green apples, crab apples,

Basics of Preserving

blackberries, cranberries, gooseberries, grapes, lemon rind, orange rind and plums. To make juice as clear as possible, strain fruit through a jelly bag twice. Allow the juice to drip at its own rate; don't squeeze the bag unless you want very thick jelly. The right amount of pectin and acids is a must. For juice rich in pectin, use 3/4 cup of sugar for each cup of juice; for juice poor in pectin, use 1/2 cup of sugar for each cup of juice. Best results come from cooking no more than four to six cups of juice at a time. Bring juice to a full boil before adding sugar. Cook over medium heat, stirring constantly, until sugar has dissolved. Then boil rapidly to retain flavor and color. Jellying point is reached when a jelly thermometer reads 220° to 222°, or when a clean wooden spoon dipped into the jelly has two large drops form along the edge, run together and fall as one drop. (This is called sheeting.)

MARMALADE

A preserve made by cooking a fruit or a combination of fruits with sugar. Citrus fruits with their rinds are most commonly used, including oranges, grapefruits, limes and lemons. The fruit, when cooked, is clear and the syrup like jelly. Citrus fruits take much longer to cook than other fruits because of the toughness of the rind, so more water is needed to compensate for evaporation.

The fruit is first soaked overnight in water twice its volume. It is then simmered for about one hour or until the rind is soft. Sugar is added at the second cooking stage in the proportion of 3/4 cup of sugar for each cup of pulp. Cook the pulp and sugar in small quantities, using four to six cups of pulp for each batch. Once the sugar has dissolved, bring the mixture to a full rolling boil. Test for jellying point with a jelly thermometer which should read 220° to 222°, or with clean wooden spoon by dipping it into the syrup to see if two large drops form along the edge, run together and fall as one drop. (This is called sheeting.) Remove the kettle from the stove and skim and stir for five minutes to prevent fruit from floating.

PRESERVES

Fruits, whole or in slices, which have been cooked slowly in syrup for preservation. In cooking preserves, it is best to do small quantities at a time, about five cups of fruit and an equal amount of sugar. If the syrup becomes too thick before the fruit is tender, add 1/4 cup of boiling water at a time. If the fruit becomes clear and tender and the syrup is still thin, remove the fruit with a slotted spoon and cook the syrup rapidly to desired consistency or almost to jellying point.

SUGGESTED
ACCOMPANIMENTS

Ham
Preserved watermelon rind
Peach butter
Red pepper jelly
White fig preserves

Corned Beef
Fig jam
Apple butter
Cherry conserve

Omelets
Strawberry jelly
Red tomato jam
Julie's mango chutney
Eunice's wine jelly

Cheese
Strawberry jam
Grapefruit marmalade
Tomato ginger preserves
Apricot butter

Chicken
Ginger pear marmalade
Red currant jelly
Apricot preserves
Drunkard's cherries (brandied)

Turkey
Cranberry jelly
Cranberry nut conserve
Loquat jam
Preserved pears

Duck
Red pepper jelly
Bar-le-duc
Green grape conserve
Kumquat preserves

Wild Game
Grape jelly
Quince jelly
Preserved Morello cherries
Apple and plum chutney

Venison
Green tomato preserves
Preserved Damascus figs
Gooseberry jelly
Apple and green tomato chutney

Goose
Guava jelly
Cherry jelly
Grape conserve
Apricot chutney

Beef
Bar-le-duc
Kiwi preserve
Crab apple jelly
Julie's mango chutney

Lamb
Lemon mint jelly
Green chili-pepper jelly
Peach chutney
Satsuma plum conserve

Veal
Concord grape jelly
Gooseberry preserves
Paul's tomato chutney
Rhubarb conserve

Pork
Tomato-apple chutney
Elderberry jelly
Apricot jam
Kumquat preserves

Indian Honey-Reed

J AM AND JELLY makers have watched the price of sugar climb with dismay, since sugar is so important to the art. In 1974, sugar prices quadrupled. We may never again see the day when, literally, sugar was cheaper than dirt. That condition applied, at least in New York City, in the mid-1950's, when a pound of dirt for the window boxes of apartment dwellers sold for 10 cents, a few cents higher than the going rate for sugar. In any event, sugar is unlikely to regain the luxury status it held in the Western world two centuries ago.

As P. L. Simmonds wrote in *Tropical Agriculture* in 1877, "The luxuries of man soon become his necessities, and he works with intense thought and labour for things of which he once was wholly ignorant. This is the case of sugar. No longer than five hundred years ago our European race did not know sugar at all. A hundred years ago it was a great luxury. Now it is sold at three pence or four pence per pound, and used in abundance as an every-day article, by the poorest people."

Mr. Simmonds' statement may have been errant by one or two hundred years. It is a matter of record that in 1226, Henry the III asked the Mayor of Winchester to procure for him three pounds of sugar "if such could be got." The same prince ordered the Sheriff of Winchester to dispatch four loaves of sugar to Woodstock. (A loaf of sugar was 10 pounds.)

Cane sugar came to Europe from India via the Middle East. It was known as the Indian honey-bearing reed; honey had been the chief sweetener in the Western world for millenia. In 1546, Sir Edward Wotton wrote Lord Cobham from Calais that imports of sugar were increasing and prices greatly reduced; a consignment of 25 loaves of sugar was available at six shillings a loaf, or 12 pence per pound. This was the price to the importer, before excise, before the profit to the apothecary; the price to the consumer, be he a belted earl or a chimney sweep, was considerably higher. Also, a consignment of 25 loaves, or 250 pounds, would scarcely alter the course of Empire. Yes, in the 16th century, sugar was so rare and believed to possess such medicinal properties that it was dispensed by apothecaries. One who lacked the necessities of life was likened to an apothecary without sugar.

The 16th century saw the introduction of sugar planting into the West Indies, which soon became its principal source. The sugarcane was dominant for two centuries, until a rival source developed, the sugar beet. Jean-Anthelme Brillat-Savarin in the gastronomic classic, *The Physiology of Taste,* remarks that with the cultivation of beet sugar, "Europe might actually, in this respect, dispense with the services of America and Hindustan." The cultivation of the sugar beet on an intensive scale had begun under Napoleon, to circumvent the Continental blockade. As an aside to his cross-Channel neighbors, Brillat-Savarin writes, "As a striking instance of the force of prejudice and of the difficulty of establishing a fact, that out of a hundred British subjects taken indiscriminately, there are not ten who believe sugar can be made from a beet-root." He notes animals are fond of sugar, "and the English, who frequently give it to their favorite horses, have observed that thus they can stand better their different trials of exertion." Later, Brillat-Savarin writes of the increasing use of sugar, mixed with water, concentrated to produce syrups, and sugar ices "said to have been introduced from Italy by Catherine de Medici." Mixed with coffee, it develops its aroma, and when milk is added, "gives a very light and pleasant food, very suitable for men of studious habits, and an especial favorite of the ladies. Mixed with fruit and the essence of flowers, it gives preserves, marmalades, candies and other confections, ingeniously retaining for us the enjoyment of their flavor and perfumes long after the time fixed as the natural limit."

Brillat-Savarin speaks of a M. Delacroix, a popular and prolific author, who used to grumble at Versailles about the price of sugar, then more than four shillings a pound. M. Delacroix vowed that if sugar were ever to sell at a shilling a pound, he would never drink water without sugar. "His prayers have been heard, and as he still lives, I suppose he keeps his word."

The Physiology of Taste, Brillat-Savarin's masterpiece, came close to being unwritten. During the Reign of Terror of the French Revolution, the author was forced to flee the country, and all that stood between him and prison and possibly the guillotine was a safe-conduct pass out of the country. He mounted his horse for Dôle, on the Swiss border, where a minor functionary named M. Prot held the life-or-death power to issue the pass. On arriving at Dôle, M. Prot was evasive, and seemed suspicious of Brillat-Savarin. A friend of the author, with some difficulty, succeeded in getting M. Prot to accept an invitation to dine with him and the would-be émigré. As it happened, Brillat-Savarin was not only an authority on *haute cuisine,* he was well grounded in all the arts. Mme. Prot accompanied her husband to the dinner, and Savarin soon discovered that she was exceedingly fond of music; there were few to share her interest in the small, provincial town. She talked of books about music; he knew them all. She discussed the operas; he had seen every one. She named the famous singers; he told of hearing their finer performances. After supper she sent for her music books, and soon they were all singing in full voice. The evening ended with Mme. Prot and Savarin singing the duet *Vous souvient-il de cette fête* from *La Fausée Magie.* At the moment of parting, Mme. Prot said, "Citizen, no one who has cultivated the fine arts as you have done can betray his country."

The next day Brillat-Savarin received his safe-conduct pass, "Duly signed and magnificently sealed," and so began three years of exile from his native land. *The Physiology of Taste* was published more than 30 years later, one year before his death in 1826.

II Butters

The Oldest Cookbook

ONLY A SINGLE cookbook comes down to us from antiquity: *De re coquinaria,* by Apicius. Few question the authenticity of the book or its recipes; although there are many questions regarding the author. There were several Roman trenchermen who bore the name Apicius, notably Marcus Apicius, who lived at the time of Sulla (circa 100 B.C.), and M. Gabius Apicius, who lived during the time of Tiberius, 14 A.D. to 37 A.D. Both of these noblemen were addicted to the pleasures of the table. Of the two, M. Gabius more probably inspired the cookbook, for his fame as a gormandizer is legendary. *De re conquinaria* is thought to have appeared about a century after Gabius' death; the book appeared under the name or psuedonym of Apicius Coelis. The recipes tend to be terse; for example, *"A Dish of Quinces:* A dish of quinces is made as follows. Quinces are cooked with leeks, honey and broth, using hot oil, or they are steeped in honey." But then brevity was always the hallmark of the Roman language, viz. Caesar's, *"Veni, vidi, vincit,"* which makes Admiral Perry's message to General Harrison after the Battle of Lake Erie, "We have met the enemy and they are ours," unduly long-winded.

Apicius does not occupy the place of Lucullus and Nero in gustatory annals, the latter, the thinly disguised Trimalchio of the *Satyricon* of Petronius Arbiter. His fame as a gourmet, however, is firmly established. The scholar Athenaeus gives us an account of M. Gabius Apicius. He was rich and lived in luxury, for the most part in the town of Minturnae in Campania. According to Athenaeus, several kinds of cheesecake were called Apician, although none of them found their way into *De re coquinaria.* Apicius spent a fortune on his stomach, and was especially fond of the very expensive crayfish of the area, which were larger than those of Smyrna, or even the crabs of Alexandria. Hearing that the crayfish of North Africa were even larger than those of Minturnae, he set sail at once, undergoing a most difficult voyage. When he came near the coast, the fishermen of North Africa pulled up beside his ship in boats loaded to the gunwales with their finest crayfish. When he saw them, Apicius asked if they had any finer. The fishermen assured him there were no finer. He promptly ordered the captain of his vessel to put about, and he returned to Italy, convinced there were no finer crayfish than those of Minturnae.

Athenaeus records another story: When the Emperor Trajan was conducting a campaign in Parthia (now northeastern Iran) many miles from the sea, Apicius sent him fresh oysters, so kept by a clever contrivance of his own. The "clever contrivance" has not come down to us, and the method of preserving oysters in the cookbook would not have done the job.

On closer scrutiny, M. Gabius emerges much more the gourmet than the glutton. His contemporaries tell us he was forever puttering about the kitchen, operating under the theory one more cook did not spoil the broth. He is said to have collected recipes as eagerly as the Victorian housewife. A part of that fortune his critics had him squandering on his belly was used to endow a school for instruction in cooking, and for advancing the culinary arts. Many of his ideas on nutrition have since been confirmed by modern science. These aspects of Apicius the man make it difficult to believe the story which has been told and retold over the centuries. When Apicius discovered that he had only 10 million *sestertii* left of his fortune, he took poison at a banquet especially convened for the occasion. That amount is equal to roughly $500,000 translated into today's wilting dollar. The tale would have us accept that Apicius took his own life for fear he might starve to death some day. It simply is not credible. Ten million *sestertii* was a considerable sum in his day. Add to this the evidence that Apicius was advancing in age, in an era when the life span was far below ours. Again citing Athenaeus, if Apicius had lived under the reigns of Tiberius (A.D. 14 through 37) and Trajan (A.D. 98 through 117), he could have been no younger than 61, probably considerably older. Yet both Seneca and Martial report the suicide in their writings, and it is repeated by Suidas, Albino and others writers as factual.

Apicius lived in an age when Rome was at the apex of its splendor and glory. The Roman Republic had become the Roman Empire, and Tiberius was the second Emperor of Rome after Augustus. The Pax Romana had been established and was to continue for 200 years. The boundaries of the empire extended to the Danube, the Middle East, across Gaul to Britain. The hostile barbarians were held at bay by the Roman legions; the 30,000 gods of the Roman pantheon had not yet given way to the single God proclaimed by Jesus of Nazareth in the province of Palestine. The recipes that come down to us through *De re coquinaria* are hardly the type to inspire the excesses of a Lucullus or a Nero. They would not be worthy props in a Cecil B. De Mille epic. They are more closely related to the frugal fare to which the freedmen and simple citizenry sat down.

SPICED APPLE BUTTER

*This is a childhood favorite
as well as one of the first preserved
sweets made in the colonies.*

6 pounds of Golden Delicious apples
1-1/4 cups of water
1/4 cup of freshly squeezed lemon juice
1/2 teaspoon of salt
1-1/2 teaspoons of ground cinnamon
1/4 teaspoon of ground cloves
3-1/2 cups of brown sugar (tightly packed)
1/2 cup of orange-flavored liqueur

Wash, quarter and core apples; it is not necessary to peel them. In a preserving kettle, combine apples, water and lemon juice; cover and simmer about 30 minutes. Remove from stove and force contents through a sieve or a food mill. Return to the kettle and add salt, cinnamon, cloves and brown sugar. Simmer, uncovered, stirring more frequently as the mixture thickens; it takes about 1-1/2 hours to thicken enough. Remove from heat and stir in liqueur. Ladle mixture into hot, sterilized jars and seal immediately according to directions in Chapter 1.
Makes approximately 8 half-pints.

APPLE BUTTER

24 medium-size apples (almost 6 pounds)
2 cups of sweet cider
3 cups of sugar (1-1/2 pounds)
1-1/2 teaspoons of ground cinnamon
1/2 teaspoon of ground cloves

Wash the apples and slice them into small pieces. Do not peel or core them. Combine apples and sweet cider in a preserving kettle, cover and cook over medium heat until apples are tender. Press pulp through a sieve to remove skins and seeds. Return pulp to kettle and add the sugar and spices. Simmer uncovered over low heat, stirring occasionally, for about 1-1/2 hours until the butter is of a spreading consistency, or until when a little is placed on a cold plate no rim of liquid separates around the edge. Ladle into hot, sterilized jars and seal at once according to directions in Chapter 1. Makes approximately 10 half-pints.

Butters

APRICOT BUTTER

The best of the butters!

5 pounds of apricots
6 cups of sugar (3 pounds)
Juice and grated rind of 1 orange

Wash and pit apricots; put through a food chopper or chop finely. In a preserving kettle, combine apricots, sugar and orange juice and rind. Cook uncovered over medium heat about 1 hour until mixture is thick enough to spread, stirring occasionally. Remove from the heat and skim off foam with a metal spoon. Ladle into hot, sterilized jars and seal immediately according to directions in Chapter 1.
Makes approximately 10 half-pints.

BETTY'S BANANA BUTTER

10 medium-size ripe bananas
5 cups of sugar (2-1/2 pounds)
Juice of 1 lemon
1 6-ounce bottle of liquid pectin

Peel and crush the bananas to a fine pulp. Place in a preserving kettle and add the sugar and lemon juice. Heat slowly until sugar has dissolved, stirring constantly. Bring to a full rolling boil and boil rapidly for 1 minute. Remove from heat and immediately stir in liquid pectin. Ladle into hot, sterilized jars and seal immediately according to directions in Chapter 1.
Makes approximately 10 half-pints.

CANTALOUPE BUTTER

A delicious spread or tart filling.

6 pounds of soft, ripe cantaloupes
1-1/2 cups of sugar
Juice of 1 lemon
1/4 teaspoon of ground nutmeg

Remove the seeds of the cantaloupes and scoop out the edible portion of the pulp. Dice the fruit coarsely and simmer, uncovered, in a preserving kettle until tender; or purée the pulp in a blender. Measure the pulp; there should be 4 cups. Return pulp to preserving kettle and add the sugar, lemon juice and nutmeg. Cook the mixture uncovered over medium heat, stirring constantly, until the butter is thick enough to spread, about 1-1/2 hours. Ladle into hot, sterilized jars and seal immediately according to directions in Chapter 1.
Makes approximately 4 half-pints.

Butters

ENGLISH LEMON CURD

Delicious over hot scones for tea.

4 large lemons
4 large eggs
1/4 pound of butter
1-1/2 cups of sugar

Wash the lemons and grate the rinds finely, eliminating all pith. Squeeze and strain the juice. Beat the eggs. In a double boiler, melt the butter, add lemon rind and juice, sugar and well-beaten eggs. Simmer the mixture, uncovered, over medium heat for about 25 minutes, or until it is smooth and creamy. Ladle into hot, sterilized jars and seal immediately according to directions in Chapter 1. This will keep about 2 months.
Makes approximately 3 half-pints.

SPICED PEACH BUTTER

Perfect with corned beef.

3 pounds of peaches
1/2 cup of water
Approximately 2-1/2 cups of sugar (1-1/4 pounds)
Juice and grated rind of 1 lemon
2 teaspoons of ground cinnamon
1 teaspoon of ground cloves
1 teaspoon of ground allspice

Wash, blanch, peel, pit and chop the peaches. Place them in a preserving kettle with the water and cook slowly until they are pulp, about 20 minutes. Press them through a sieve or purée in a blender and measure pulp. There should be about 5 cups. Return pulp to the preserving kettle and add 1/2 cup of sugar for each cup of purée. Then add the grated lemon rind and juice, cinnamon, cloves and allspice. Cook slowly, uncovered, for about 45 minutes, or until thick enough to spread. Ladle into hot, sterilized jars and seal immediately according to directions in Chapter 1.
Makes approximately 8 half-pints.

SPICED PEAR BUTTER

6 pounds of firm, ripe pears (Anjou or
    Bosc are best)
1-1/4 cups of water
1/4 cup of freshly squeezed lemon juice
1/2 teaspoon of salt
1-1/2 teaspoons of ground cinnamon
1/4 teaspoon of ground cloves
3-1/2 cups of brown sugar (tightly packed)
1/2 cup of port

Wash, core and quarter unpeeled pears. Put fruit in a preserving kettle with the water and lemon juice. Cover and simmer about 30 minutes until fruit is soft. Remove from the stove and force pulp through a food mill or sieve. Return pulp to the kettle and add salt, cinnamon, cloves and sugar. Cook slowly uncovered, stirring frequently, until mixture thickens, about 1-1/2 hours. Remove from the stove and stir in port. Ladle into hot, sterilized jars and seal immediately according to directions in Chapter 1.
Makes approximately 8 half-pints.

PRUNE BUTTER

Can be made and used on toast on cold winter mornings when all other fruits have gone "underground."

2 pounds of dried pitted prunes
Approximately 2 cups of sugar
1/4 teaspoon of ground cinnamon
1/4 teaspoon of ground cloves
1/4 teaspoon of ground allspice

Cook the prunes in a little water until they are soft. Mash thoroughly, then sieve or blend them. Measure the pulp into a preserving kettle and add 1/2 cup of sugar for each cup of pulp. Add spices and cook mixture slowly, uncovered, until the butter is a spreadable consistency, about 30 minutes. Ladle into hot, sterilized jars and seal immediately according to directions in Chapter 1. Makes approximately 5 half-pints.

Butters

RHUBARB BUTTER

2 pounds of rhubarb
1/2 cup of water
2 cups of sugar (1 pound)
Red food coloring

Wash and cut up the rhubarb; do not peel if the skin is tender. Cover with the water in a preserving kettle. Simmer uncovered until tender, about 15 minutes. Strain the pulp. Return pulp to the heat, and bring slowly to a boil, stirring in the sugar. Continue stirring until the sugar has dissolved. Cook uncovered, stirring occasionally, until the mixture is thick and creamy, about 1 hour. Add a few drops of food coloring, ladle into hot, sterilized jars and seal immediately according to directions in Chapter 1.
Makes approximately 4 half-pints.

TOMATO BUTTER

8 pounds of tomatoes
6-1/2 cups of brown sugar (tightly packed)
1 tablespoon of ground cinnamon
1 tablespoon of ground cloves
1 teaspoon of ground allspice

Wash the tomatoes and cut them into quarters; put them into a preserving kettle. Cook uncovered over medium heat until soft, about 20 minutes. Put tomatoes through a sieve, return to kettle and add the brown sugar, cinnamon, cloves and allspice to the pulp. Simmer uncovered about 45 minutes, or until thick enough to spread. Ladle into hot, sterilized jars and seal immediately according to directions in Chapter 1.
Makes approximately 16 half-pints.

TOMATO-APPLE BUTTER

5 pounds of tomatoes
1-1/2 pounds of tart, green apples
4-1/2 cups of sugar (2-1/4 pounds)
2 cups of cider vinegar
1 stick of cinnamon
1 tablespoon of grated ginger root
1 teaspoon of ground nutmeg
1 tablespoon of whole cloves

Wash, blanch, peel and slice the tomatoes. Wash, peel, core and slice the apples. Place these in a preserving kettle with sugar and the vinegar. Tie the spices in a cheesecloth bag and add to the kettle. Simmer uncovered for about 1-1/2 hours until the mixture thickens to spreading consistency, stirring occasionally (especially during the last 30 minutes of cooking time). Remove cheesecloth bag. Ladle into hot, sterilized jars and seal immediately according to directions in Chapter 1. Makes approximately 11 half-pints.

Washington's Cherry Blossoms

MASON LOCKE WEEMS, better known as Parson Weems, is responsible for that enduring bit of American folklore that George Washington, as a child, chopped down a cherry tree. When pressed by his father, he admitted it after exclaiming, "I cannot tell a lie." Weems was indeed a parson; he had been ordained a deacon in England and pursued his ministry in his native United States. He was also an author of sorts; in 1800, a year after the President died, Weems rushed into print *History of the Life and Death, Virtues and Exploits of George Washington.* Literary historians report it was not until the book entered its fifth edition that Weems introduced the story of the cherry tree. Weems was the precursor of the semi-fictional biographers so popular in our times. His "history" of Washington was to be followed by biographies of Francis Marion (the Swamp Fox), Benjamin Franklin, and William Penn, all of them more the product of the Parson's imagination than of factual evidence.

The apochryphal nature of Parson Weems' tale of George Washington and the cherry tree hardly squares with the nature of his subject. Given a choice, the president would rather be remembered as George Washington: Farmer, than as Washington: Soldier, Statesman and Founder of His Country. Agriculture he regarded as "the most honorable pursuit of man." His one wish during his public life was to retire to Mt. Vernon and the farming life. In 1788, he wrote his English correspondent, Arthur Young, Esq., "I can only say for myself, that I have endeavored, in a state of tranquil retirement, to keep myself as much from the eye of the world as I possibly could. . . . For I wish most devoutly to glide silently and unnoticed through the remainder of my life. This is my heart-felt wish; and these are my undisguised feelings."

His wish was unfulfilled. A few months after this letter, the Constitution of the United States was adopted, a federal government was formed, and he was chosen first President of the United States, a position he held until two years before his death. The seat of the federal government was in New York, moving to Philadelphia in 1890, which kept him away from his beloved Mt. Vernon for long periods. He wrote William Strickland after retiring from the Presidency, apologizing for not writing the Englishman sooner, ". . . for at no time have I been more closely employed in repairing the ravages of an eight years' absence. Engaging workmen of different sorts, providing and looking after them, together with the necessary attention to my farm, have occupied all my time since I have been at home."

Washington rhapsodized in a letter to Young about Mt. Vernon, "no estate in America is more pleasantly situated than this. It lies in a high, dry and healthy country, three hundred miles by water from the sea, and as you will see by my plan [map], on one of the finest rivers in the world."

The president was critical but understanding of the problems of the American farmer. In 1791, he wrote Young, "The aim of the farmers in this country, if they can be called farmers, is not to make the most they can from the land, which is, or has been, cheap, but the most of labour, which is dear; the consequence of which has been much ground has been *scratched* over and not cultivated or improved as it ought to have been; whereas a farmer in England, where land is dear and labour is cheap, finds it in his interest to improve and cultivate highly, that he may reap large crops from a small quantity of ground."

In that same year, Washington enumerated the tax rates on property in Virginia. The tax on Negro slaves was two shillings sixpence (six shillings to the dollar), while the tax on chariots (coaches) was nine shillings sixpence per wheel. The formidable tax on coaches may have been an attempt to divert citizens to the horse, waterways or shanks-mare due to the imperfect state of the road-building art. Or it may simply have been a tax on the affluent, in those distant days before the income tax and loopholes for the rich.

George Washington kept slaves. In his last will and testament he decreed that upon the death of his wife, Martha, the slaves were to be freed, and that the young or the old and infirm among them were to be provided for by his family.

Washington over the years kept a diary of his farming activities. We find these entries on May 1, 1762, when he was 30. "Grafted 10 Carnation Cherries, on growing stock in the garden—Viz., 5 of them in and about the Mint Bed, 3 under the Marsella Cherry tree, 1 on a stock in the middle of the border of the last square. . . . 1 other on a stock just above the 2nd gate. . . .

"Grafted 6 Early May duke Cherry's on the nursery, begin'g at that end of the first Row next to the Lane. . . .

"Also Grafted joining to those in the same Row 6 of the latter May dukes—which are all the Cherry in the Row. Also Grafted 7 Bullock Heart Cherrys in the last Row."

Although the cherry was only a minor crop in Washington's vast holdings—69,615 acres of land, 24 city lots and one whole city square—the tender care shown in the entries above dispells the impression of a person, even as a lad, who would go about hacking down cherry trees, as Weems would have us believe.

III Chutneys

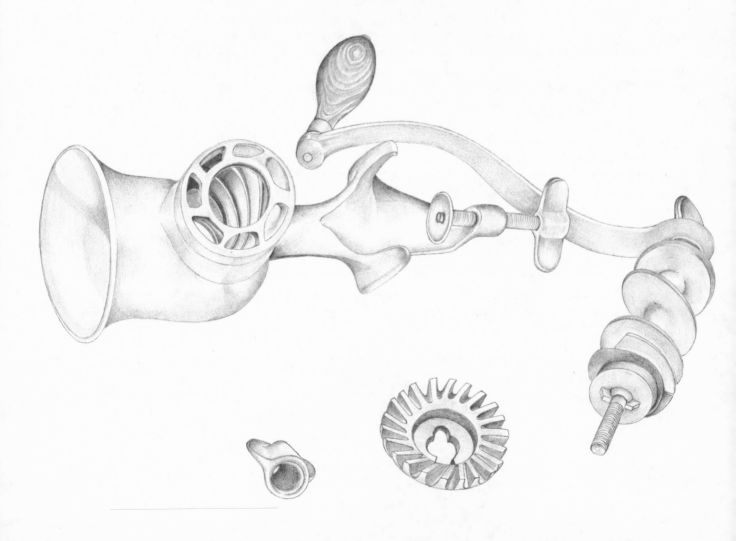

Elusive Major Grey

THE WORD CHUTNEY derives from the Hindu *katni* or *chatni,* and is not, as widely supposed, a contraction of a London suburb. Chutney to many people outside of India means Major Grey's. Inside India Major Grey is unknown, on no less authority than the estimable writer Santha Rama Rau. Grey's memory, however, is preserved in a quatrain by John F. Mackay, entitled *Rank Injustice.*

> All things chickeny and mutt'ny
> Taste far better when served with chutney.
> This is the mystery eternal:
> Why didn't Major Grey make colonel?

Crosse & Blackwell's, the well-known purveyors of relishes to the Western world, insists there was a Major Grey. Chutney was the aristocrat of condiments among the princes and potentates of India. In the 18th century, British military units were entertained by these local rulers and this led to the introduction of chutney to Britain and the world. According to Crosse & Blackwell: "One of these officers, a Major Grey, was also a gourmet. He adapted one of the Indian chutney recipes and began a commercial production of the item in India. He later contacted Crosse & Blackwell, already established as a packer of quality food specialties, to produce and sell the product in England and elsewhere."

This particular chutney became so popular that other condiment makers copied the ingredients as nearly as they could, and even included the name Major Grey with their brand names. So today Major Grey indicates a type of chutney, although Crosse & Blackwell insists theirs is the original.

India and the East Indies supplied most of the ingredients for C & B's chutney until the Japanese cut the supply lines in World War II. Since then, the company has turned to the Caribbean for its mangoes, tamarinds, limes, ginger and flavorings. The spices are still imported from the East Indies. We must add that no self-respecting Indian family will serve a preserved chutney. Their chutney is prepared fresh, *al dente,* for the forthcoming meal. There are prepared and preserved chutneys sold in India, as elsewhere, but they are not for consumption by the finer palates. Major Grey is *persona non grata* in the better households.

The name Major Grey is associated with curries among Westerners. The Indians regard the Western version of curry with horror: a mixture of flour and yellow cream sauce served with meat, fish or chicken on a bed of rice, with Major Grey's chutney as a topping. An example is the curry of Mr. Arnot of Greenwich, in *Apician Morsels,* by Humelbergius Secundus. "Take the heart of a cabbage, that is the very inside, and nothing but the inside, pulling off all the leaves until it is the size of an egg; chop this very fine; two apples in thin slices, the juice of one lemon; half a teaspoonful of black pepper; one teaspoonful of

Cayenne pepper, one *large* teaspoonful of *my* curry powder." Mr. Arnot's own curry powder consists of eight ounces of turmeric, four ounces of coriander seed, two ounces of "cummin" seed, and two ounces of "foenigreck" seed "to be separately powdered and finely mixed."

After mixing the above ingredients together well, Mr. Arnot instructs us to add six onions, a finely chopped garlic, butter, flour, a pint of meat gravy, roasted fowl or rabbit, or lean chops of pork or mutton, or a lobster, or the remains of yesterday's calf's head, or anything else you may fancy. "Mark, that in this way, you may curry anything—old shoes would even be delicious, some old oil-cloth, or stair carpet not to be found fault with—(gloves, if much worn, are too rich)—Oh, send it up warm—a warm-water dish is worth a diadem." There follows rice. Needless to say, Mr. Arnot's curry would be a capital offense in India.

No mention of mango in the above recipe, unthinkable to the Indian taste. No mango, no chutney, since the mango is the heart of chutney. The reason for being of the curries of India is the unbearable heat of the summer; the torrid curries on their staple fare are a coolant. In the dessicating heat of the summer, the Indians look forward to two things: the monsoon and the mango season. The mango season is short and the rainy monsoon season long. Sometimes it is a question of which comes first, the mangoes or the monsoon. If the monsoon arrives before the mango ripens, the fruit is lost. Usually the mango beats out the monsoon, and Indian women are busily pickling mangoes to last until the next season. Come the monsoon and its arrival is celebrated in South India with the festival of Devi, the wife of Lord Shiva; there are celebrations, processions, painted elephants, camels and horses. The occasion is the more festive if the mangoes are harvested, pickled and stored against the rainy season.

Major Grey? In India, he is as well known as Gungha Din.

APPLE AND PLUM CHUTNEY

Gorgeous with pork, ham or cheeses.

1-1/2 pounds of apples
2-3/4 pounds of plums
1 pound of onions
2 cups of seedless raisins
2 cups of cider vinegar
2-2/3 cups of brown sugar (tightly packed)
1 tablespoon of salt
1 teaspoon of ground ginger
1 teaspoon of ground allspice
1/4 teaspoon of ground nutmeg
1/4 teaspoon of cayenne pepper
1/4 teaspoon of ground cloves
2 teaspoons of whole mustard seeds

Wash, peel, seed and dice apples; wash, seed and dice the plums; peel and chop the onions finely. Combine these with all remaining ingredients in a preserving kettle and bring to a boil over medium heat. Lower the heat and simmer the mixture, uncovered, for about 2 hours. When it is rich and thick, ladle into hot, sterilized jars and seal immediately as directed in Chapter 1.
Makes approximately 6 half-pints.

APPLE CHUTNEY

Good with ham or pork.

4 pounds of cooking apples
1 lemon
1 clove of garlic
2-1/4 cups of brown sugar (tightly packed)
1-1/2 cups of seedless raisins
3/4 cup of crystallized ginger
1-1/2 teaspoons of salt
1/4 teaspoon of cayenne pepper
2 cups of cider vinegar

Wash, peel, core and chop apples. Wash, seed and chop the lemon; peel and chop the garlic clove. In a preserving kettle combine the apples, lemon and garlic with brown sugar, raisins, crystallized ginger, salt, cayenne pepper and cider vinegar. Simmer this mixture, uncovered, for about 2 hours. Ladle into hot, sterilized jars and seal immediately according to directions in Chapter 1.
Makes approximately 6 half-pints.

Chutneys

APPLE AND GREEN TOMATO CHUTNEY

*This is an old, East Indian
chutney made by the British.*

12 tart green apples (Gravenstein or Pippin)
24 small green tomatoes
4 medium-size onions
3 cups of seedless raisins (1 pound)
4 cups of cider vinegar
2-1/2 cups of brown sugar (tightly packed)
2 tablespoons of salt
1/2 teaspoon of crushed, dried red
   chili peppers
1-1/2 tablespoons of curry powder
3 tablespoons of mixed pickling spices

Wash, core and chop the apples; wash, blanch, peel and chop the tomatoes and chop the onions. Place apples, tomatoes and onions in a preserving kettle and add raisins, vinegar, sugar, salt, red peppers and curry powder. Put the pickling spices in a cheesecloth bag and add to the kettle. Boil, stirring occasionally, for 25 minutes, or until apples are transparent. Remove fruit with a slotted spoon. Boil syrup rapidly until it thickens. Discard pickling spices, return the fruit to the syrup and bring to a boil. Remove from the heat and ladle into hot, sterilized jars and seal immediately according to directions in Chapter 1.
Makes approximately 24 half-pints.

APRICOT CHUTNEY

Delicious with pork or curries.

3-1/2 pounds of large, firm apricots
4 sweet red peppers (or green may be used)
1 orange
1 lemon
3 onions
1 clove of garlic
1 cup of seedless raisins
4-1/2 cups of brown sugar (tightly packed)
1-3/4 cups of cider vinegar
1/2 cup of coarsely chopped crystallized ginger
1 teaspoon of salt
1 teaspoon of ground ginger
1 cup of chopped blanched almonds

Wash the apricots, peppers, orange and lemon. Pit and chop the apricots; seed and chop the peppers, orange and lemon; peel and chop the onions and garlic; chop the raisins. Set aside. (All of these ingredients may be put through a food chopper.) Boil the sugar and vinegar in a preserving kettle for 5 minutes. Add the apricots, peppers, orange, lemon, onions, garlic, raisins, crystallized ginger and salt. Cook uncovered about 35 minutes, stirring frequently. Now add ground ginger and almonds and cook another 30 minutes. Ladle into hot, sterilized jars and seal immediately according to directions in Chapter 1.
Makes approximately 6 half-pints.

APRICOT AND DATE CHUTNEY

Since the fruits in this recipe are dried,
it can be made at Christmas for gift-giving.

2 pounds of dried apricots
2-1/2 cups of pitted dates
1 cup of preserved ginger
3 cups of white wine vinegar
2-1/2 cups of brown sugar (tightly packed)
3 cups of white seedless raisins (1 pound)
3 teaspoons of salt
3 tablespoons of whole mustard seeds
1 teaspoon of chili powder
2 cups of water

Soak the apricots in water to cover for 30 minutes. Then drain and place them in a preserving kettle. Chop the dates and the ginger and add to the apricots. Combine the vinegar, sugar, raisins, salt, mustard seeds, chili powder and water and add to the mixture. Simmer the chutney over low heat for 2 hours. Ladle it into hot, sterilized jars and seal immediately as directed in Chapter 1.
Makes 8 half-pints.

BANANA GINGER CHUTNEY

This may be used with meats or
with sour cream in crêpes.

12 ripe bananas (about 3 pounds)
2 pounds of Bermuda onions
2 cups of pitted dates (1 pound)
2/3 cup of molasses
1 cup of water
1/2 teaspoon of ground ginger
2 cups of cider vinegar
1 teaspoon of ground allspice
1 teaspoon of salt

Peel and cut the bananas and onions into small pieces; chop the dates into small pieces. Combine the bananas, onions and dates with remaining ingredients, mixing well. Turn mixture into a stone casserole or crock and cook this mixture, uncovered, in a 325° oven until it is a rich brown in color, about 1 hour. Ladle into hot, sterilized jars and seal immediately according to directions in Chapter 1.
Makes approximately 11 half-pints.

Chutneys

GOOSEBERRY CHUTNEY

4 pounds of gooseberries
3 medium-size onions
3 cups of brown sugar (tightly packed)
1-1/2 cups of cider vinegar
1-1/2 cups of dry, white wine
1 cup of seedless raisins
1 teaspoon of salt
2 teaspoons of dry mustard
1 teaspoon of ground ginger
1 teaspoon of turmeric
1/2 teaspoon of cayenne pepper

Wash the gooseberries and remove the stems and blossoms. Chop or grind the gooseberries and onions together and place them in a preserving kettle with the remaining ingredients. Cook this mixture uncovered over low heat, stirring frequently, until it thickens, about 2 hours. Ladle into hot, sterilized jars and seal immediately according to directions in Chapter 1.
Makes approximately 8 half-pints.

GUAVA CHUTNEY

*Perfect for curries or meats
and delicious in avocado halves.*

6 pounds of guavas
5 medium-size onions
2 cloves of garlic
3 cups of cider vinegar
3 teaspoons of ground cinnamon
2 teaspoons of ground cloves
4 teaspoons of ground allspice
5 cups of sugar (2-1/2 pounds)
3 tablespoons of salt
1/2 teaspoon of crushed, dried red chili peppers

Wash and seed the guavas and put them through a meat grinder or chop into small pieces. Peel and chop or grind the onions and garlic. Put all the ingredients into a preserving kettle. Place the kettle, uncovered, over low heat and simmer until mixture is rich and thick, about 2 hours. Ladle into hot, sterilized jars and seal immediately according to directions in Chapter 1.
Makes approximately 12 half-pints.

KIWI CHUTNEY

12 kiwi berries
3 medium-size onions
1 lemon
3/4 cup of seedless raisins
1-1/2 cups of cider vinegar
1-1/2 cups of brown sugar (tightly packed)
1/4 cup of coarsely chopped preserved ginger
1 teaspoon of ground ginger
1-1/2 teaspoons of salt
1/4 teaspoon of cayenne pepper

Wash, peel and quarter the kiwi berries and place them in a preserving kettle. Peel and finely chop the onions; wash, slice and seed the lemon and chop the raisins. Combine these ingredients with remaining ingredients and add to the preserving kettle. Place uncovered over low heat and simmer gently, stirring frequently, for 1-1/2 hours, or until mixture is reduced to a smooth pulp. Ladle into hot, sterilized jars and seal immediately according to directions in Chapter 1.
Makes approximately 7 half-pints.

JULIE'S MANGO CHUTNEY

This mango chutney beats any you can buy.

10 large mangoes
2 cloves of garlic
1 onion
1 cup of seedless raisins
1 cup of cider vinegar
1 cup of freshly squeezed lime juice
1-1/2 cups of brown sugar (tightly packed)
1/2 teaspoon of crushed, dried red chili peppers
1 tablespoon of celery seeds
1 tablespoon of whole mustard seeds
2 tablespoons of grated fresh ginger root
1-1/2 teaspoons of salt

Wash, pare, seed and cut mangoes into small pieces and put them into a crock or bowl. Peel and chop the garlic and onion and add to crock with all remaining ingredients. Cover and let mixture stand overnight. The next morning, put this mixture into a preserving kettle and cook slowly, uncovered, for about 3 hours, or until thick. Ladle into hot, sterilized jars and seal immediately according to directions in Chapter 1.
Makes approximately 10 half-pints.

Chutneys

QUICK NECTARINE CHUTNEY

A must with beef curry!

3 pounds of ripe nectarines
1 medium-size onion
1 cup of seedless raisins
1/2 cup of cider vinegar
Juice of 2 lemons
1/4 cup of slivered preserved ginger
1 teaspoon of ground allspice
1/2 teaspoon of ground cinnamon
1/2 teaspoon of ground cloves
1/2 teaspoon of ground ginger
1 tablespoon of salt
1/4 cup of powdered pectin
1-1/2 cups of brown sugar (tightly packed)
3 cups of white sugar (1-1/2 pounds)

Wash, blanch, peel and seed the nectarines and slice them into a preserving kettle. Peel and finely chop the onion and add to the kettle with raisins, vinegar, lemon juice, preserved ginger, allspice, cinnamon, cloves, ground ginger, salt and pectin. Mix thoroughly, bring to a boil and boil rapidly for 15 minutes. Add sugars and cook 5 more minutes. Ladle into hot, sterilized jars and seal immediately as directed in Chapter 1.
Makes approximately 10 half-pints.

PEACH CHUTNEY

6 pounds of firm peaches
1 sweet green or red pepper
3 cups of seedless raisins (1 pound)
1 clove of garlic
Piece of ginger root the size of a walnut
1 quart of cider vinegar
4 cups of brown sugar (tightly packed)
1/4 cup of whole mustard seeds
1 tablespoon of salt
Juice of 1 lemon

Wash, blanch, peel and pit peaches; cut up into small pieces. Remove seeds and membrane from the pepper and finely chop or put through a food grinder with the raisins, garlic clove and ginger root. Add to the peaches and set aside. Now make a syrup by boiling the vinegar, sugar, mustard seeds, salt and lemon juice together. Add the fruit mixture to the syrup and simmer uncovered about 2-1/2 hours until thick and transparent. Ladle into hot, sterilized jars and seal immediately according to directions in Chapter 1.
Makes approximately 10 half-pints.

PEAR AND GINGER CHUTNEY

3 pounds of Bartlett pears
1 pound of onions
Juice and grated rind of 1 orange
Juice and grated rind of 1 lemon
1 cup of brown sugar (tightly packed)
1/2 cup of seedless raisins
1 cup of cider vinegar
1/2 teaspoon of ground cloves
1 teaspoon of ground ginger
1 teaspoon of salt
1/2 teaspoon of crushed, dried red chili peppers

Wash, peel, core and chop the pears; peel and chop the onions. Put pears and onions in a preserving kettle and add all remaining ingredients, mixing well. Bring the mixture to a boil; then simmer uncovered for about 2 hours or until thick. Ladle into hot, sterilized jars and seal immediately according to directions in Chapter 1.
Makes approximately 6 half-pints.

Chutneys

PAUL'S TOMATO CHUTNEY

5 pounds of ripe tomatoes
5 cups of brown sugar (tightly packed)
2-1/2 cups of cider vinegar
1 tablespoon of whole cloves
1 tablespoon of ground allspice
1 stick of cinnamon
3 cups of seedless raisins (1 pound)

Wash, blanch, peel and chop the tomatoes and place them in a preserving kettle with the sugar and vinegar. Tie spices into a cheesecloth bag and add to mixture. Boil slowly, uncovered, for about 2 hours. Add the raisins and boil 1 hour longer. Remove and discard the spice bag. Ladle the mixture into hot, sterilized jars and seal immediately according to directions in Chapter 1.
Makes approximately 10 half-pints.

TOMATO-APPLE CHUTNEY

Excellent complement to any cold meat.

5 pounds of tomatoes
4 pounds of green cooking apples
1/4 cup of preserved ginger
1-1/2 cups of chopped onion
3/4 cup of chopped green pepper
6 tablespoons of whole pickling spices
1/4 teaspoon of crushed, dried red chili peppers
1 cup of seedless raisins
2 teaspoons of salt
2-1/2 cups of brown sugar (tightly packed)
2 cups of cider vinegar

Wash, blanch, peel and chop the tomatoes. Peel, core and chop the apples. Chop the ginger into fine pieces. Put the tomatoes and apples in a preserving kettle and add ginger, onion and green pepper. Put the pickling spices and chili pepper into a cheesecloth bag and add this with the raisins, salt, sugar and vinegar to the tomato mixture. Bring slowly to a boil and simmer uncovered for 2-1/4 hours, or until thick. Remove the spice bag and discard it. Ladle into hot, sterilized jars and seal immediately as directed in Chapter 1.
Makes approximately 14 half-pints.

The Short, Happy Life of Mrs. Beeton

THE IMAGE of the author which arises upon reading *Mrs. Beeton's Book of Household Management* is of a stout, bosomy, tightly stayed middle-aged woman in complete command of the domestics upstairs, downstairs and the 'tweenies, an uncompromising mistress of the kitchen and the larder, the giver and the protectress of the laws for daily living in Victorian England. Her maxims were so widely respected that the book became the favored gift to thousands of newly married young housewives.

The image could not be farther from the mark. The book was published when the author was 24 years old, and was the compilation of three years of monthly articles begun when she was 21. The articles had appeared in *The Englishwoman's Domestic Magazine,* one of a stable of magazines which her husband published, most of them successful. Mrs. Beeton was beautiful and, according to her contemporaries, vivacious, chatty and witty. Much of the *Book of Household Management* was devoted to recipes, for in the words of Isabella Beeton, "I have always thought that there is no more fruitful source of family discontent than a housewife's badly cooked dinners and untidy ways." Which leads to other Beetonisms, "A place for everything and everything in its place," and "Clean as you go, for muddle makes more muddle."

The book, published by her husband, was an instant success, and in its first year sold 60,000 copies. While preparing the monthly articles of which the book was the sum of their parts, a friend, Mrs. English of Newmarket, was sceptical of the project. "Cooking is a science that is only learned by long experience and years of study which of course you have not had." But Mrs. English later introduced Mrs. Beeton to Mr. Orpwood, cook for the Duke of Rutland, as well as to the chief cook for Lord Wilton. And Mrs. English imparted to Mrs. Beeton a secret known to great chefs everywhere: "You will find that the stockpot is the secret of the kitchen. Without it, nothing can be done; with it, everything can be done."

Many of the recipes in Mrs. Beeton's book came solicited or unsolicited from readers of *The Englishwoman's Domestic Magazine.* Others she picked up from friends. Her recipe for baroness pudding, a suet pudding liberally sprinkled with raisins, was given her by the Baroness de Tessier, an émigré living in Epsom. (Mrs. Beeton's stepfather, Henry Dorling, printed race cards for the Epsom track and was lessee of the Grand Stand at Epsom.) Her *soupe à la cantatrice,* principally composed of eggs and sago (a starch also used for stiffening cloth), honored Jenny Lind, "the Swedish nightingale," as soup was supposedly soothing to the singing voice.

After the book appeared, some of Mrs. Beeton's friends complained that their husbands asked, "Why can't you cook like Mrs. Beeton?" Mrs. Beeton's reaction was uncompromising; she invited these friends and their husbands for dinner at her home, and served up an execrable meal, to teach the husbands not to criticize their wives.

One of Mrs. Beeton's less-inviting recipes is labeled *Useful Soups for Benevolent Purposes,* made from ox head, meat bones, leeks, celery, turnips and beer. This she distributed to the poor families in Pinner in the hard winter of 1858. The children of the poor came with cans to be filled with the soup. Mrs. Beeton could not help noticing that each week the children came with bigger cans. The *Useful Soups,* she felt, gave many poor families a warm, digestible meal in place of the cold meat and piece of bread which was the usual meal of far too many cottagers. With a little more knowledge of the cooking art, they might have a warm dish every day at less expense.

Isabella Beeton even had a "receipt" for the Tony pig, or Anthony, so named because it was always the one assigned to the church at tithing time. St. Anthony was the patron saint of husbandry, and it was the practice of the herdsmen to give the scrawniest, most hapless of each 10 pigs to the kirk. Hardly a tribute to the good St. Anthony, but an example of peasant cunning, for which read survival.

The *Book of Household Management* was much more than a book of receipts. It was a wide-ranging work, advising the reader how to set a proper table or the correct way of bleeding a victim of some sudden overindulgence. In bleeding, she admonished, "a person should be bled standing or sitting up. If he faints, he can be lain down flat and the bleeding stopped. But if he is already in the flat position, he cannot be placed lower than he at present is—except, as is most likely the case, under the ground."

There were frequent passages on manners and morals. "In former times, when the bottle circulated freely among the guests, it was necessary for the ladies to retire earlier than they do at present, for the gentlemen of the company soon became unfit with that decorum which is essential in the presence of ladies. Thanks, however, to the improvements in modern society, temperance is, in these happy days, a striking feature in the character of a gentleman." This did not prevent her from including in her receipts "Mrs. Beeton's Tipsy Cake," known in America as the Tipsy Parson. The ingredients: a slightly stale sponge cake; sufficient sweet wine or sherry to cook it; six tablespoons of brandy; slivered blanched almonds; whipped cream.

Mrs. Beeton's husband, Samuel Orchart Beeton, was one of the more successful publishers in the British Isles. His earliest coup was bringing to press an early British edition of Harriet Beecher Stowe's, *Uncle Tom's Cabin.* It had a great success; eventually one-half million copies were sold, of which Beeton's press churned out about 200,000 copies. The impetus of the Stowe book placed him in the vanguard of British publishers. Gratefully, he voyaged to America to present Mrs. Stowe with a voluntary payment of 500 pounds; under existing copyright laws, he was not legally bound to do so. Subsequently, he sent her another 250 pounds.

As his series of magazines prospered, he moved to grander quarters at 248 The Strand, "10 doors from the Temple Bar" as his advertisements proclaimed. His trademark was "The Sign of the Bee-Hive," illustrated to suit. And a bee-hive it was: Mrs. Beeton not only did the monthly *Household Management* column for the *The Englishwoman's Domestic Magazine,* but also did the fashion column for it and subsequent magazines. The fashion column required of her at least two trips a year to Paris, not only to view the spring and fall showings of the couturiers, but to secure the detailed, colored engraved plates for reproduction in her husband's magazines.

No, Mrs. Beeton was not a bosomy, bustled, grey-haired dispenser of advice on careful domestic economy. The truth is all too tragic. The Beetons had lost their first two children in their infancy. The third was a healthy, lusty boy. Mrs. Beeton was revising and correcting proofs on a foreshortened version of the *Book of Household Management,* entitled *Mrs. Beeton's Dictionary of Everyday Cooking,* during her fourth confinement. She gave birth to a brawling, hearty lad and was ecstatic her sturdy third son had a brother. So he did, for he survived for many years, but on the second day following the birth, Mrs. Beeton, who had never been sick a day of her life, developed puerperal fever, and within a week was dead. She was 28.

Her grieving husband wrote as an epilogue to the posthumous *Dictionary of Everyday Cooking:* "... Cold in the silent tomb lie the once useful, nimble fingers—now nerveless, unable for anything, and ne'er to do work more in this world. Exquisite palate, unerring judgment, sound common sense, refined taste—all these had the dear lady who has gone 'ere her youth had scarcely come ... for her duty no woman has ever better accomplished than the late

ISABELLA MARY BEETON."

Samuel Beeton did not survive his wife by too many years. He and his publishing house were brought down in the collapse of the great banking house of Overend, Gurney, on May 10, 1866, a "Black Friday" comparable to the "Black Tuesday" of October 29, 1929, in the United States. The *Times* described it as a "national disaster," and it was adjudged the greatest financial crisis ever to hit the City of London. Beeton sold his copyrights, signed on as a literary advisor to a rival firm, and died of tuberculosis on June 6, 1877.

IV Conserves

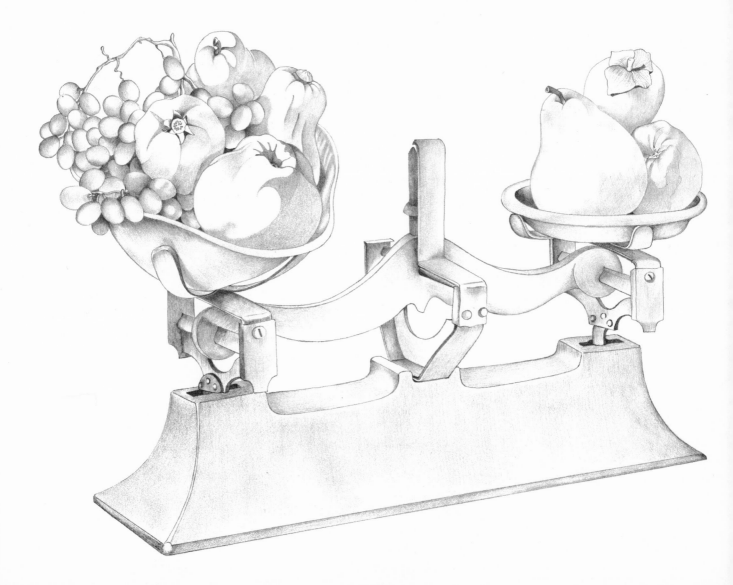

The Doctor and the Lady

D R. SAMUEL JOHNSON enjoyed the company of women, yet his opinions on them were condescending or to a feminist, slanderous. His most often quoted pronouncement is, "Sir, a woman preaching is like a dog's walking on his hind legs. It is not done well, but you are surprised to find it done at all." The good doctor obviously didn't anticipate Aimee Semple McPherson. On another occasion he avowed a woman could not write a good book of cookery, a canard, since most good books of cookery have been written by women. The remark was made at a dinner given by the publisher Dilly at which Anna Seward, Boswell and several others were at table. Boswell quotes Johnson as boasting, "I could write a better book about cookery than has ever yet been written; it should be a book upon philosophical principles. Pharmacy may be so, too. A prescription, which is now compounded of five ingredients, had formerly fifty in it. So in Cookery. If the nature of the ingredients is well known, much fewer will do. Then, as you cannot make bad meat good, I would tell what is the best butcher's meat, the best beef, the best pieces; how to choose young fowls; the proper seasons of different vegetables; and then how to roast, and boil, and compound."

Dilly: "Mrs. Glasse's 'Cookery,' which is the best, was written by Dr. Hill. Half the trade knows this."

Johnson: "Well, Sir, that shows how much better the subject of cookery may be treated by a philosopher. I doubt if the book be written by Dr. Hill; for in Mrs. Glasse's 'Cookery,' which I have looked into, saltpetre and salt-prunella are spoken of as different substances, whereas salt-prunella is only saltpetre burnt on charcoal, and Hill could not be ignorant of this. However, as the greatest part of such a book is made by transcription, this mistake may have been carelessly adopted. But you shall see what a book of cookery I could make. I shall agree with Mr. Dilly for the copyright."

Miss Seward: "That would be Hercules with the distaff indeed!"

Johnson: "No, Madam. Women can spin very well; but they cannot make a good book of cookery."

Hannah Glasse's thin volume was published in 1747. It was entitled *The Art of Cookery, Made Plain and Easy, which far Exceeds Every Thing of the Kind Ever yet Published . . . By a Lady. London: Printed for the Author; and sold at Mrs. Ashburn's, a China Shop, the Corner of Fleet Ditch.* Mrs. Glasse was the wife of a London attorney. She was not without her prejudices, particularly against French chefs. "If gentlemen will have French cooks, they must pay for French tricks." At another point she writes, "A Frenchman, in his own country, would dress a fine dinner of twenty dishes, and all genteel and pretty, for the expense he will put an English Lord for dressing one dish. But then there is a little petty profit. I have heard of a cook that used six pounds of butter to fry 12 eggs, when every one knows that a half a pound is enough. . . . But then it would not be French. So much is the blind folly of this age, that they would rather be imposed upon by a French booby, than give encouragement to a good English cook."

Like many cookbooks published since her time, recipes for foods were followed by a section on home remedies. The most interesting is her "Receipt for the Plague." It is a witches' brew, compounded of many ingredients. How Mrs. Glasse procured the receipt is curious. During the Great Plague there were four villainous "malfactors" who robbed infected houses and murdered the people inside. When finally captured and brought to the gallows, they gave the receipt she reprinted as the only medicine they used to preserve them from contagion, and they went from house to house without any fear of distemper.

Hannah Glasse's injunction against French cooks was largely ignored in the century and a half that followed. The *chef de cuisine* for Queen Victoria was a Frenchman, Charles Elme Francatelli. He was a pupil of the great Carême, who as chef for Talleyrand is given credit for much of that diplomat's success at the Congress of Vienna. Carême went on to become the head cook for English Prince Regent (later George IV), for Czar Alexander I of Russia, and for the Baron de Rothschild. Francatelli wrote a cookbook himself, "Adapted for the use of all families, large or small, as well as for Hotels, Restaurants, Cooks, Bakers, Clubs and Boarding Houses. . . ." In it are several observations on English cookery. Among them is "the excess of quantity and variety of spices and condiments are the bane of English cooking."

Later Francatelli grows ruminative. "England possesses a greater abundance of all kinds of foods, generally of far better quality than is to be found elsewhere, yet our cookery, in theory and practice, has become a by-word of ridicule . . . that we should be compelled to have recourse to foreigners, ignorant for the most part of our tastes and habits, to prepare our feasts." Coming from the pen of a foreigner whom Queen Victoria had recourse to, the words have a strange ring. But so strongly did Francatelli embrace his British citizenship, so smartly did he salute the Union Jack, he was every inch the Englishman, one of the "we," while the Continent he had left behind was the land of the "they."

CHERRY CONSERVE

5 pounds of Bing cherries
1 orange
Juice of 1 lemon
4 cups of sugar (2 pounds)
1 cup of chopped almonds or pecans
1 cup of seedless raisins

Wash and pit cherries; wash, thinly slice and seed the orange. Put cherries and orange slices into a preserving kettle and add the lemon juice and sugar. Cook the mixture, uncovered, about 45 minutes, stirring frequently until it is thick and transparent. Remove from the stove. Skim off the foam with a metal spoon; then add the nuts and the raisins and cook another 10 minutes. Ladle into hot, sterilized jars and seal immediately according to directions in Chapter 1.
Makes approximately 5 half-pints.

CRANBERRY NUT CONSERVE

This makes a beautiful Christmas present.

2 pounds of cranberries
1 orange
1 cup of seedless raisins
3 cups of sugar (1-1/2 pounds)
1/2 cup of chopped pecans

Wash cranberries. Cover with water and cook them until they pop. Then press cranberries through a food mill or mash them thoroughly. Wash, seed and finely chop the orange; chop the raisins. Combine the cranberries, orange and raisins in a preserving kettle and cook slowly, uncovered, for 10 minutes. Add the sugar and simmer gently, stirring frequently, until thick, about 20 minutes. During the last 10 minutes of cooking time, add the pecans. Ladle into hot, sterilized jars and seal immediately according to directions in Chapter 1.
Makes 9 to 10 half-pints.

Conserves

HELENA'S YULETIDE WHOLE CRANBERRIES

Perfect with domestic fowl or wild game.

2 pounds of cranberries
2 cups of sugar (1 pound)
1/2 cup of water
1/2 orange, including rind
3 whole cloves
1/2-inch stick of cinnamon
1/2 cup of cognac

Wash the cranberries and set aside. In a preserving kettle, boil the sugar and water for 3 minutes. Wash, seed and finely chop the orange half and add with the cranberries, cloves and cinnamon stick to the preserving kettle. Boil this mixture until the cranberries pop, about 6 minutes. Stir in the cognac. Ladle into hot, sterilized jars and seal immediately according to directions in Chapter 1. Makes approximately 4 half-pints.

ENGLISH CUCUMBER AND GINGER CONSERVE

You are in for a crunchy, delicious surprise!

4 large English cucumbers
8 cups of sugar (4 pounds)
Piece of ginger root the size of a lemon

Peel and thinly slice the cucumbers; cover with sugar and let stand for 24 hours. Strain the cucumber juice and sugar into a preserving kettle, reserving the cucumber slices, and simmer the juice gently until the sugar dissolves. Tie the ginger into a cheesecloth bag and bruise it with a hammer. Add the bag to the syrup and boil for 45 minutes. Add the cucumber slices and boil for 10 minutes. Leave mixture in the preserving kettle and let it stand, covered, for 12 hours. Boil the mixture hard for 15 minutes; remove and discard the ginger. Ladle the conserve into hot, sterilized jars and seal immediately according to directions in Chapter 1. Makes approximately 12 half-pints.

GOOSEBERRY AND PINEAPPLE CONSERVE

*Cover plain cookies
with this for a tea-time treat.*

3 pounds of gooseberries
1/2 cup of water
2 cups of shredded pineapple (canned pineapple
  may be used if rinsed lightly in water)
2 cups of seedless raisins
4 cups of sugar (2 pounds)
2 cups of chopped pecans

Wash and remove blossoms and stems from the gooseberries. In a preserving kettle, boil the gooseberries in the water until they burst, about 10 to 12 minutes. Add the pineapple and cook for 10 minutes, stirring constantly. Add the raisins and sugar. Simmer uncovered for about 15 minutes, stirring frequently. Add the pecans and cook for 5 minutes to heat them through. Ladle into hot, sterilized jars and seal immediately according to directions in Chapter 1.
Makes approximately 9 half-pints.

Conserves

GREEN GRAPE CONSERVE

2 medium-size oranges
4 lemons
2 limes
3 cups of water
3 pounds of seedless grapes
6 cups of sugar (3 pounds)
2 tablespoons of seedless raisins
1/2 cup of coarsely chopped walnuts

Wash, seed and chop the oranges, lemons and limes. Barely cover them with the water and boil for 10 minutes in a preserving kettle. Wash and stem the grapes and add to the fruit in the kettle with the sugar and raisins; simmer for 40 to 50 minutes, until the mixture is thick and jellied. Add walnuts and remove from the heat. Ladle into hot, sterilized jars and seal immediately according to directions in Chapter 1.
Makes approximately 8 half-pints.

HARLEQUIN'S CONSERVE

2 pounds of strawberries
2-1/2 pounds of cherries
1 large ripe pineapple
1 large orange
3/4 pound of seedless grapes
6 cups of sugar (3 pounds)
1 cup of coarsely chopped walnuts or pecans

Wash and hull the strawberries. Wash the cherries and remove the pits and stems. Peel, core and dice the pineapple. Peel, seed and dice the orange. Wash and stem the grapes. Place the prepared fruits in a preserving kettle and cover with the sugar; cover and let stand overnight. The next day, bring the mixture to a boil over medium heat, lower the heat and simmer uncovered until clear and thick, about 45 minutes to 1 hour. Add walnuts or pecans and cook for 2 minutes. Ladle into hot, sterilized jars and seal immediately according to directions in Chapter 1.
Makes approximately 12 half-pints.

CAROL'S PEACH CONSERVE

Peachy with pound cake
for an emergency dessert.

4 pounds of peaches
2 oranges
6-3/4 cups of sugar (approximately 3-1/2 pounds)
1 cup of coarsely chopped walnuts

Wash, blanch and peel the peaches; remove the pits and dice the fruit into a preserving kettle. Peel, seed and chop the 2 oranges; reserve the rind of 1 of the oranges and slice it into thin strips. Add orange pulp and rind and sugar to the preserving kettle. Boil over medium heat, stirring frequently, until the mixture is thick, about 30 to 40 minutes. Then add the walnuts and cook 10 more minutes. Ladle into hot, sterilized jars and seal immediately according to directions in Chapter 1.
Makes approximately 9 half-pints.

PEAR CONSERVE

5 pounds of underripe pears
10 cups of sugar (5 pounds)
2 cups of seedless raisins
Finely grated rind of 2 oranges
Juice of 3 oranges
Juice of 2 lemons
3/4 cup of coarsely chopped walnuts

Wash, peel, core and dice the pears. Cover them with the sugar and let stand overnight. The next morning, place pear mixture in a preserving kettle and add raisins, orange rind and orange and lemon juice. Simmer uncovered, stirring constantly, about 1 hour until thick. Then add the walnuts and cook for 5 minutes. Ladle into hot, sterilized jars and seal immediately according to directions in Chapter 1.
Makes approximately 12 half-pints.

Conserves

SATSUMA PLUM CONSERVE

4 pounds of Satsuma plums
6 cups of sugar (3 pounds)
3 cups of seedless raisins (1 pound)
1 cup of water
Grated rind and juice of 1 orange
1 cup of chopped walnuts

Wash, pit and coarsely chop plums. Put them into a preserving kettle with sugar, raisins, water and orange rind and bring to a boil. Simmer uncovered for 30 minutes, stirring frequently. Add orange juice and simmer for 25 more minutes. Skim off foam with a metal spoon. Add nuts and simmer 5 minutes. Remove from heat, ladle into hot, sterilized jars and seal immediately according to directions in Chapter 1.
Makes approximately 12 half-pints.

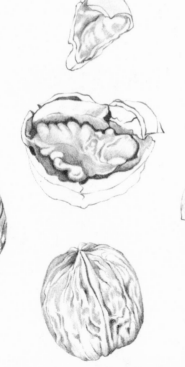
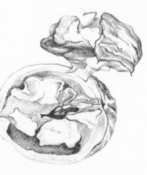

RED RASPBERRY CONSERVE

Delicious with brioches or croissants.

2-1/2 pounds of red raspberries
1 pound of currants
4-1/2 cups of sugar (2-1/4 pounds)
1/4 cup of freshly squeezed orange juice

Wash and drain the raspberries; set aside. Wash the currants and simmer them in a preserving kettle over low heat until the juice is extracted, about 15 minutes. Add the raspberries and heat to the boiling point, stirring constantly. Add the sugar and orange juice and cook this mixture over medium heat for 40 minutes until thickened, stirring frequently. Ladle into hot, sterilized jars and seal immediately according to directions in Chapter 1. Makes approximately 12 half-pints.

RHUBARB CONSERVE

3-1/2 pounds of rhubarb
4 ounces of candied orange peel
6 cups of sugar (3 pounds)
Juice and grated rind of 2 lemons
1 cup of slivered blanched almonds

Wash, peel and cut the rhubarb into 1/2-inch pieces. (If the skin is very tender, do not peel.) Shred the candied orange peel. Put rhubarb and shredded peel into a preserving kettle and add sugar, lemon rind and juice. Bring slowly to a boil and stir until sugar has dissolved. Then simmer uncovered for 40 minutes. Add the almonds and cook 5 more minutes. Ladle into hot, sterilized jars and seal immediately according to directions in Chapter 1.
Makes approximately 5 half-pints.

Conserves

GREEN TOMATO CONSERVE

This gives your leftover meats a lift!

2 medium-size lemons
16 green tomatoes
1-1/2 pounds of tart apples
1-1/2 cups of water
3 cups of sugar (1-1/2 pounds)
1 2-inch stick of cinnamon
1/2 teaspoon of whole cloves
1 tablespoon of mixed pickling spices

Wash the lemons. Peel them lengthwise, shave the peel and seed and chop the pulp. Boil the peel in the water for 30 minutes; drain the peel and set peel and pulp aside. Wash the tomatoes and parboil them for 7 minutes; then dice them. Wash, peel, core and dice the apples and place them in a preserving kettle with the sugar, lemon pulp and tomatoes. Tie all of the spices into a cheesecloth bag and add to the fruit. Boil the mixture for 20 to 25 minutes, stirring frequently. Remove and discard the spice bag and continue to simmer the pulp for 20 minutes. Add the reserved lemon peel to the mixture and cook for an additional 20 minutes. Remove from the stove and ladle into hot, sterilized jars and seal immediately according to directions in Chapter 1.
Makes approximately 7 half-pints.

PRESERVED WATERMELON RIND

A must for ham!

6 cups of watermelon rind
4 tablespoons of salt
2 quarts of cold water
1 tablespoon of ground ginger
4 cups of sugar (2 pounds)
1/4 cup of freshly squeezed lemon juice
7 cups of water
1 lemon

Trim the green skin and pink pulp from the thick watermelon rind. Cut the trimmed rind into 1-inch squares and measure out 6 cups. Dissolve the salt in the 2 quarts of cold water and soak the melon rind overnight. Drain the rind and rinse well; then add water just to cover and let stand 30 minutes; drain again. Sprinkle the rind with ginger, cover it with water and simmer, uncovered, for about 15 minutes, or until it is tender when pierced with a fork. Drain the rind and set it aside. Boil together the sugar, lemon juice and 7 cups of water in a preserving kettle for 5 minutes. Add the melon rind and cook for 30 minutes more. Slice the lemon wafer-thin and discard the seeds. Add lemon slices to the melon rind and syrup and boil the mixture until the rind is clear and transparent. Ladle into hot, sterilized jars and seal immediately according to directions in Chapter 1.
Makes approximately 6 half-pints.

Johnny Appleseed

THE BOOK OF GENESIS makes no reference to the apple. It speaks only of "the fruit of the tree" which the Lord God had commanded Adam and Eve not to eat. The only fruit in the Garden of Eden for which there is textual evidence is the fig, for having eaten of the forbidden fruit, "the eyes of them both were opened, and they knew that they were naked; and they sewed fig leaves together, and made themselves aprons."

Since America grows, eats, bakes and generally ingests more apples than any other country, let us begin our story in the early days of the American Republic. It was in the spring of 1798, when New England-born John Chapman worked his way west with small quantities of appleseed in his deerskin knapsack. He first edged into history sowing seed for an apple nursery in western Pennsylvania. This was the beginning of Johnny Appleseed, who holds a permanent place in American folklore. How much of his story was myth and how much real we shall never know. His tale was transmitted as oral history and the frontier people who passed it on are long under the sod.

Johnny moved his seedling tree nurseries along with the expanding American frontier. In 1801, he was in the Territory of Ohio, where he planted a nursery on the borders of Licking Creek. He gathered his seeds from the pomace of western Pennsylvania cider presses, carrying them by horse or by foot for distances up to 150 miles.

His love of animals earned him the name of the American St. Francis. He once found a wolf caught in a trap and badly hurt. Johnny Appleseed nursed it back to health, made a pet out of it, and the beast followed him around like a dog until some misguided rustic shot it. A friend saw John walking one foot bare and one foot shod, and asked the reason for the bare foot. Replied Johnny, "It offended me. It trod on a worm and crushed it, and I am going to punish it." On another occasion he doused a campfire for fear of singeing a cloud of mosquitoes. When clearing a road through a forest with other settlers, he destroyed a hornets' nest. One got underneath Johnny's famed coffee-sack coat, and stung him repeatedly. The wilderness St. Francis gently removed the hornet. When asked why he did not kill the hornet, John answered, "It would not be right to kill the poor thing, for it did not intend to hurt me." He upbraided a squirrel hunter for taking the life of the poor creature, as God was the author of all things.

Johnny was not vain about his appearance; placed beside him, some of his fellow frontiersmen might have stepped out of a New York salon. He is portrayed as a small, wiry man, with long, dark hair and a scanty beard which he never shaved, and keen black eyes. It was his custom to wear cast-off clothes, often thrust upon him by settlers in exchange for his apple seedlings. On his head, he wore a tin mushpot, which he later discarded for a cardboard headcover with a broad beak to protect his face from the sun. More than one border child was frightened when he burst from the forest into a clearing. In his late years he favored tow-linen coffee sacks with holes cut out for his arms and his head, "a very serviceable cloak, and as good clothing as any man need wear." He never ate meat, and spurned coffee, tea and tobacco, but was partial to milk and honey because "We read that this is heavenly food."

In his early travels, he preferred the hammock strung between two trees in the wilderness to a lodging, a habit acquired from the Indians. Indians treated Johnny Appleseed with great respect, by reason of his honesty and his openness. On his part, he blamed the hostility of the Indians toward the settlers on the white man's cupidity. For the Indians he was a man apart; they never harmed him and he ranged the wilderness with impunity, even though he often forewarned settlers of Indian raids, bursting into cabins and shouting, "The Spirit of the Lord is upon me, and he hath anointed me to blow the trumpet in the wilderness and sound the alarm in the forest; for, behold, the tribes of the heathen are round about your doors, and a devouring flame follows them."

Recent, more diligent research, sorting fact from fancy, concludes it would be wrong to portray Johnny as an eccentric, impoverished philanthropist. Records show that in 1815 he had 640 acres of land under lifetime leases and owned outright two town lots in Mt. Vernon, Ohio. Yet he is known to have been uncomfortable with money, and is said to have sold the seedlings from his nurseries for notes payable at some indefinite date in the future. Many of them went uncollected. Or he disposed of funds to pay for the wintering of old and lame horses, which he gathered up after they had been turned loose by their owners in the wilderness. Other monies he gave to struggling families hard-pressed by the exegencies of border life.

With his appleseeds and seedlings, Johnny carried into the westering borders a fervent evangelism, in the form of the teachings of Swedenborg. He entered the wilderness cabins proclaiming "Fresh news from Heaven" and would proceed to read from the Swedenborg Bible or distribute Swedenborgian tracts. When asked why he never married, a rather obtuse question in light of his appearance, he told of his frequent conversations with angels and spirits, two of them who would become his wives in Heaven if he remained unmarried on earth. He believed the next world would be a continuation of life on earth, and people would have the same occupations. When a listener asked, "Do you think people will die in the next world?" Johnny replied, "I think not." To which the listener replied, "Then my occupation is gone, for I am a gravedigger."

The story most repeated about Johnny the Evangelist concerns an itinerant parson, well dressed for a frontiersman, preaching to a gathering from his pulpit atop a tree stump. He decried the lack of Christian virtues among the crowd gathered around him, exhorted them to better ways at peril of fire and brimstone, and with passion asked the question, "Where now is the man who, like the primitive Christian, is traveling to heaven barefooted and clad in coarse raiment?" Johnny Appleseed bestirred himself from the log on which he had been reclining, placed his bare foot upon the stump of a pulpit, pointed to his coffee-sack garment, and said quietly, "Here is your primitive Christian."

Thanks to John Chapman, more than 100,000 square miles of apple orchards are estimated to have sprung up in the Middle West, from western Pennsylvania to Illinois. Every spring the apple blossoms bloom in tribute to our folk hero. Johnny Appleseed expired on a visit to a country cabin near Fort Wayne, Indiana, at age 72. Witnesses said they had never seen a man more placid in the face of death. He had good reason: By his beliefs he was about to meet the two wives he thought were waiting for him, and since a man continued his former occupation after death, the pastures of Heaven became the fertile soil for him to plant his seeds, tend his nurseries, and plant apple orchards without limit.

V Jams

Whistle While You Pick

"**I**T IS WELL to instruct children picking berries to whistle as they pick." This bit of mother wit has been passed on for generations, for the minute the children stop whistling, you may be sure they are eating berries. And who is to blame them? A fresh, or well preserved, berry is among the tastiest of foods.

At the top of the list is the strawberry. Ike Walton, in *The Compleat Angler,* states: "Indeed, my good Scholar, we may say of Angling, as Dr. Boteler said of strawberries: 'Doubtless God could have made a better berry, but doubtless God never did.'" Grimond de la Reynière, in his *Almanach des Gourmands,* agrees. "The most precious fruit which the divine Providence provides for our tables, and which Paris regards as one of the most distinguished, is the strawberry."

The long season of the strawberry makes it doubly blessed, extending from the end of April into late September and beyond. De la Reynière continues, "The fruit is as healthy as it is pretty. It is woodsy, refreshing, a little laxative it is true; but when seasoned with sugar and wine, this property is overcome, and it is made the friend of almost all stomachs. . . . The strawberry is eaten raw, with powdered sugar, and sometimes with a little wine. We have tried to make compotes, jams, etc., but until now without success. The fire removes almost all its bouquet. Meanwhile M. Henrion, confectioner, rue Vivienne, has made a confection of whole strawberries, which is not to be disdained [*dédaigner*]." De la Reynière will have no quarrel with our translation; he is long gone.

The strawberry is a ground berry; among the bushberries, the raspberry is the most widely cultivated. The botanical name of the raspberry, *Rubus idaeus,* refers to the raspberries growing on the slopes of Mount Ida in Asia Minor, at the foot of which lay the city of Troy. So the berry has been with us for a long time. Although it has been cultivated since at least the fourth century, Stephen Switzer in 1724 mentioned only three kinds as under cultivation in England. By 1829, George W. Johnson mentions 23 varieties of plants. Like other berries, the raspberry was thought to have medicinal properties, and Gerard Dewes' translation of *Dodoen's New Herball,* published in 1587, lists the following "vertues."

"The flowers of Rapsis are good to be brused with hony, and layde to the inflammations and hoate humours gathered togither in the eyes, and Erysipelas or wilde fire, for it quencheth such hoate burnings.

"They be also good to be dronken with water of them that have weak stomachs.

"The framboye [raspberry] is founde in some places in Douchland in darke woods: and in this Countrie they plante it in gardens, and it loveth shadowye places, where the Sonne shineth not often."

When the raspberry was first cultivated in the United States, the foreign variety was preferred to the native plants. It was later discovered the foreign plants were not as able to withstand the extremes of the climate of North America. So the *Rubus strigosus*, native American, came into its own.

The blackberry, or bramble to the Europeans, also has long been prized for its medicinal qualities. The eminent physician Boerhave, in the early 19th century, prescribed that its root be dug in February and March and boiled with honey to make an excellent remedy for dropsy. Again quoting the Dewes' translation of Dodoen, who was physician to the German emperor, "They do also fasten the teeth, when the mouth is washed with the juyce or decoction thereof. . . . The leaves be stamped & with good effect are applyed to the region or place of the stomacke against the trembline of the heart, the payne & looseness or ache of the stomacke."

The blackberry is the thorniest of the bushberries, and therein lies a legend. According to the naturalist Charles Waterton, "The Cormorant was once a wool merchant. He entered into partnership with the Bramble and the Bat, and they freighted a large ship with wool; she was wrecked and the firm became bankrupt. Since that disaster the Bat skulks about till midnight to avoid his creditors, the Cormorant is forever diving into the deep to discover its foundered vessel, while the Bramble seizes hold of every passing sheep to make up its loss by stealing the wool."

There is another berry that is tart, palatable when modified with sugar, yet so closely linked to the turkey that its appearances are seasonal. It appears in quantity on Thanksgiving Day and Christmas, most often in canned form. The cranberry was first known as the crane berry, as it was favored by the cranes living in New England's bogs. Ships putting in at New England ports used it as a preventative of scurvy, and stowed casks of the "bogland medicine" in their stores. In colonial times, the cranberry was also known as the bounce berry, as it was tested for ripeness by its ability to bounce. And still is. Though native to New England, cranberries are now also grown commercially in New Jersey, Wisconsin, Oregon and Washington.

The berry fruits are more often used to make jams than jellies, since they do not of themselves have enough pectin and need quantities of sugar to see them through the winter. In colder climes, such as Russia, the jams are thicker and more solid than the English or American. The Russian jam is not pulped but preserved whole; the Russians do not use the jam as a spread but serve it in small glass dishes or saucers to be eaten with a spoon with tea. Preserving and pickling are an art with the Russians because of their long winters. In pre-Revolution literature, we read of apples, pears, grapes and cherries being pickled as they seasoned. The cooks and their helpers worked continuously during the summer preparing for the Russian winter which invaders have come to respect; the aroma of pickling spices, mushrooms, cucumbers or cabbages filling the kitchen and the whole house. The coming of the heat preserving process has shortened the work span, but not the winter.

AMBROSIA JAM

3 pounds of peaches
1 medium-size cantaloupe
1 8-1/2-ounce can of crushed pineapple
3 large oranges
1 lemon
Approximately 10-1/2 cups of sugar (5-1/4 pounds)

Wash, blanch, peel and pit the peaches and chop them into small pieces. Seed and scoop out the pulp from the cantaloupe; chop the pulp into small pieces. Drain the crushed pineapple. Seed the oranges and lemon and put through a meat grinder or chop. Measure all the fruit into a bowl and add 3/4 cup of sugar for each cup of pulp; let mixture stand overnight. The next morning, put the mixture into a preserving kettle and cook over high heat, stirring frequently, for 35 minutes, or until jellying point is reached. Test for jellying point with a jelly thermometer which should read 220° to 222°, or with a wooden spoon which, when dipped into the syrup, has 2 drops form, come together and fall as 1 drop. Pour into hot, sterilized jars and seal immediately according to directions in Chapter 1.
Makes approximately 14 half-pints.

APRICOT JAM

Here you are serving preserved sunshine on the breakfast table.

3-1/2 pounds of apricots
1 lemon
6 cups of sugar (3 pounds)

Wash and pit apricots and dice or put them through a food chopper. Squeeze the juice from the lemon and grate half of the rind. Place the rind, juice, sugar and apricots in a preserving kettle. Place over medium heat, stirring constantly, until the sugar has dissolved. Bring to a boil and boil hard, uncovered, stirring frequently, until the mixture is thick, about 20 to 25 minutes. Skim off the foam with a metal spoon, if needed. Ladle into hot, sterilized jars and seal immediately according to directions in Chapter 1.
Makes approximately 6 half-pints.

Jams

DRIED APRICOT-PINEAPPLE WINTER JAM

Delicious with hot toast or muffins with tea on a December day.

2 cups of dried apricots
2 cups of crushed pineapple (if using canned, drain)
Juice of 1/2 lemon
4 cups of sugar (2 pounds)

Wash the apricots; cover them with cold water and let soak overnight. The next morning, simmer apricots and soaking water in an uncovered preserving kettle until tender. Mash with a potato masher and then add pineapple, lemon juice and sugar. Simmer until sugar has dissolved, stirring frequently; then cook over high heat until thick, about 30 minutes. Skim off foam with a metal spoon, if needed. Ladle into hot, sterilized jars and seal immediately as directed in Chapter 1.
Makes approximately 4 half-pints.

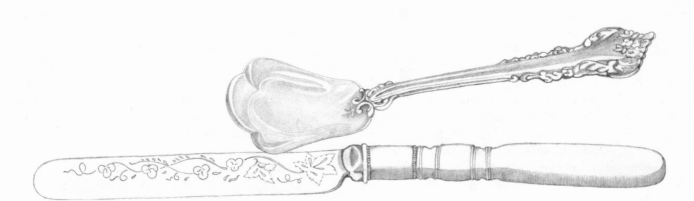

SUNSHINE APRICOT JAM

A great favorite with Southwesterners.

3-1/2 pounds of ripe apricots
Approximately 5 cups of sugar (2-1/2 pounds)

    Wash and pit apricots. Cut away any blemishes, but do not peel them. Chop apricots coarsely; measure them and place in a preserving kettle. For each well-packed cup of fruit (there should be about 5 cups), measure out 1 cup of sugar. Add sugar to apricots and cook uncovered over low heat until the sugar has dissolved. Pour fruit mixture into 1/2-inch-deep shallow pans or platters. Cover with a sheet of glass or saran wrap, propping the cover up to leave about 1 to 2 inches between the pan and cover for evaporation. Place pans in the sun and stir thoroughly 2 or 3 times a day; bring them in each night. It takes 2 or 3 days, depending on the heat of the sun, for the mixture to reach the desired thickness. Stir thoroughly and pour into hot, sterilized jars and seal immediately according to directions in Chapter 1.
Makes approximately 5 half-pints.

BLACKBERRY JAM WITH ORANGE

3 pounds of blackberries
7 cups of sugar (3-1/2 pounds)
3/4 cup of freshly squeezed orange juice
3 tablespoons of freshly squeezed lemon juice
Grated rind of 1 orange
1 6-ounce bottle of liquid pectin

    Wash the blackberries. In a preserving kettle, cook them until they are heated through. Divide them in half and put half of the berries through a sieve. Return the sieved berries to the kettle with the whole berries and add the sugar, orange juice, lemon juice and orange rind. Stir the mixture over high heat until it comes slowly to a rolling boil. Boil, stirring constantly, for 1 minute. Remove from the heat and immediately stir in the liquid pectin; then skim off foam with a metal spoon. Stir and skim for 5 minutes to prevent the fruit from floating. Ladle into hot, sterilized jars and seal immediately according to directions in Chapter 1. Makes approximately 8 half-pints.

Jams

BLUEBERRY JAM

*Sunday morning breakfast treat
with cream cheese and English muffins.*

5 pounds of fully ripened blueberries
Juice of 1 lemon
6 cups of sugar (3 pounds)

Wash, stem and crush the blueberries. Put them into a preserving kettle with the lemon juice and sugar. Bring to a boil slowly (takes about 20 minutes), stirring occasionally until sugar has dissolved. Now cook rapidly almost to jellying point, about 220° on a jelly thermometer; this takes about 30 minutes. As the mixture thickens, stir frequently. Skim off foam with a metal spoon, if needed. Ladle into hot, sterilized jars and seal immediately according to directions in Chapter 1. Makes approximately 8 half-pints.

CHERRY JAM

An all-American favorite.

3 pounds of Bing cherries
Juice of 2 lemons
1/4 cup of powdered pectin
5 cups of sugar (2-1/2 pounds)

Wash, stem and pit cherries and put them through a food chopper or cut finely. (This makes about 4-1/2 cups.) Put them into a preserving kettle with the lemon juice and the pectin and mix well. Place over high heat and stir mixture until it comes to a hard boil; immediately add sugar and bring slowly again to a full rolling boil, stirring until sugar has dissolved. Boil hard for 1 minute, stirring constantly. Remove from the stove and skim off foam with a metal spoon. Ladle into hot, sterilized jars and seal immediately according to directions in Chapter 1.
Makes approximately 7 half-pints.

DAMSON PLUM JAM

2 pounds of Damson plums
3 cups of sugar (1-1/2 pounds)
3/4 cup of water

Wash, chop and pit plums. Put them into a preserving kettle, add sugar and water and bring slowly to a boil until sugar has dissolved. Now cook rapidly almost to jellying point, 220° on a jelly thermometer. This takes about 30 minutes. As mixture starts to thicken, stir constantly to prevent sticking. Skim off foam with a metal spoon, if needed. Ladle into hot, sterilized jars and seal immediately according to directions in Chapter 1. Makes approximately 6 half-pints.

FIG JAM

2 pounds of ripe, black figs
Juice of 2 lemons
8 cups of sugar (4 pounds)
1 6-ounce bottle of liquid pectin

Wash and remove stems and ends from figs. Crush thoroughly and put into a preserving kettle, adding the lemon juice and the sugar. Mix well and bring slowly to a full rolling boil over high heat, stirring constantly. Boil hard for 1 minute. Remove from the stove, stir in the pectin and then skim off the foam. Pour into hot, sterilized jars and seal immediately according to directions in Chapter 1. Makes approximately 12 half-pints.

Jams

GOOSEBERRY JAM

An old-fashioned delight!

3 pounds of fully ripe gooseberries
1/4 cup of powdered pectin
7 cups of sugar (3-1/2 pounds)

Wash, stem and remove the blossoms from gooseberries. Chop or put them through a meat grinder. Put the fruit into a preserving kettle with the pectin and mix thoroughly. Place over high heat until the fruit comes to a hard boil, then immediately stir in sugar and bring slowly again to a full rolling boil, stirring until sugar has dissolved. Boil hard for 1 minute. Remove from the stove and skim off the foam with a metal spoon. Ladle into hot, sterilized jars and seal immediately according to directions in Chapter 1.
Makes approximately 8 half-pints.

CONCORD GRAPE JAM

*This is what Paul Revere used
for energy to start him on his ride.*

4 pounds of ripe Concord grapes
1 cup of water
7-1/2 cups of sugar (3-3/4 pounds)
1/4 cup of powdered pectin

Squeeze the pulp from the grape skins into a preserving kettle, reserving the skins. Add the water to the kettle and simmer, covered, for 5 minutes. Strain the pulp to remove the seeds and return to kettle. Grind the reserved skins and add them to the strained pulp. Stir in the sugar and pectin and bring slowly to a full rolling boil. Boil hard for 1 minute, stirring constantly. Remove from heat and stir and skim for 5 minutes. Ladle into hot, sterilized jars and seal immediately according to directions in Chapter 1.
Makes approximately 10 half-pints.

GUAVA JAM

A delicious spread for hot breads.

5-1/2 pounds of guavas
4 cups of sugar (2 pounds)
1 cup of water
1/4 cup of freshly grated lemon rind

In a preserving kettle simmer the sugar and water for 25 minutes, or until a jelly thermometer reads 220° to 222°, or the syrup sheets when dropped from a spoon (2 drops coming together and falling as 1 drop). While the syrup is cooking, wash the guavas, cut them in half and remove the seeds. Barely cover them with water and simmer, uncovered, about 20 minutes. Remove the fruit with a slotted spoon and cut into small chunks or put through a food grinder. Combine this pulp with the syrup and lemon rind in the kettle and simmer uncovered until thick, about 45 minutes, stirring frequently. Skim off foam with a metal spoon, if needed. Ladle into hot, sterilized jars and seal immediately as directed in Chapter 1.
Makes approximately 10 half-pints.

LOQUAT JAM

Lovely on pancakes!

4 pounds of ripe loquats
Juice of 2 lemons
3-1/2 cups of sugar (1-3/4 pounds)

Wash and seed the loquats, removing blossoms, stems and imperfections. Put through a meat grinder or dice them. Barely cover the fruit with water and cook until tender, about 45 minutes. Add the lemon juice and sugar and cook over medium heat, stirring frequently, until sugar has dissolved. Then bring to a rapid boil and boil about 30 minutes, stirring frequently, until jellying point is reached, 220° to 222° on a jelly thermometer, or when mixture sheets from a spoon (2 drops coming together and falling as 1 drop). Skim off foam with a metal spoon, if needed. Ladle into hot, sterilized jars and seal immediately according to directions in Chapter 1.
Makes approximately 4 half-pints.

Jams

MANGO JAM

A deliciously different flavor.

4 fully ripe mangoes
6 cups of sugar (3 pounds)
Juice of 1 large lemon
1 6-ounce bottle of liquid pectin

Peel and remove seeds from mangoes. Chop fruit thoroughly or put through a meat grinder. Place the fruit in a preserving kettle and add the sugar and lemon juice. Slowly bring to a boil over high heat and boil hard for 1 minute. Remove the jam from the heat and stir in the liquid pectin immediately. Skim off the foam with a metal spoon; then stir and skim for several minutes to keep the fruit from floating. Ladle into hot, sterilized jars and seal immediately according to directions in Chapter 1.
Makes approximately 9 half-pints.

PAPAYA-LIME JAM

*Use when the weather is warm
and dream of the tropics.*

3 pounds of papayas
1/3 cup of freshly squeezed lime juice
2 tablespoons of pineapple juice
5 cups of sugar (2-1/2 pounds)

Wash, peel and seed papayas and put through a food grinder or dice. Place fruit in a preserving kettle and cook uncovered until thickened, about 20 minutes, stirring frequently. Add the lime and pineapple juices and sugar to the kettle and cook until this mixture thickens again, stirring frequently, about 20 minutes. Skim off foam with a metal spoon, if needed. Ladle into hot, sterilized jars and seal immediately according to directions in Chapter 1.
Makes approximately 10 half-pints.

PERSIMMON JAM

3 pounds of ripe persimmons
7 cups of sugar (3-1/2 pounds)
Juice of 2 lemons
1 6-ounce bottle of liquid pectin

Wash, peel and seed the persimmons; then mash them. Place persimmon pulp in a preserving kettle, add the sugar and lemon juice and mix well. Bring slowly to a boil over high heat until sugar has dissolved, stirring frequently. Boil hard for 1 minute, then remove the kettle from the heat and stir in the liquid pectin. Skim thoroughly with a metal spoon. Ladle into hot, sterilized jars and seal immediately according to directions in Chapter 1.
Makes approximately 8 half-pints.

71

Jams

PEACH JAM

This gives a real fillip to vanilla ice cream,
or can be used to heighten
the delight of fresh peach ice cream.

3 pounds of peaches
Juice of 1 lemon
1/4 cup of powdered pectin
6 cups of sugar (3 pounds)

Wash, blanch, peel and pit the peaches. Mash or grind them thoroughly with the lemon juice. Measure 4 cups of the pulp into a preserving kettle and add the pectin, mixing thoroughly. Place this over high heat and bring to a boil, stirring constantly to avoid scorching. Add the sugar and mix well. Continue stirring and bring slowly to a full rolling boil. Boil this mixture for exactly 1 minute. Remove from heat and skim with a metal spoon. Ladle into hot, sterilized jars and seal immediately according to directions in Chapter 1.
Makes approximately 7 half-pints.

HAWAIIAN PEACH JAM

1 pound of dried peaches
1 medium-size fresh pineapple
Approximately 3 cups of sugar (1-1/2 pounds)
1/2 tablespoon of freshly grated lemon rind
1 tablespoon of freshly grated orange rind
1 tablespoon of freshly grated lime rind

Soak the peaches overnight in water; drain them. Peel and core the pineapple. Put the 2 fruits through a meat grinder or chop them, reserving the juice. Measure the fruit and juice into a preserving kettle. (There should be about 4 cups.) Add 3/4 cup of sugar for each cup of fruit mixture. Cook the fruit pulp and sugar over medium heat until the sugar has dissolved, stirring frequently. Add the citrus fruit rinds and bring to a boil. Cook uncovered over high heat for 30 to 35 minutes, stirring frequently. Skim off foam with a metal spoon, if needed. Ladle mixture into hot, sterilized jars and seal immediately as directed in Chapter 1.
Makes approximately 6 half-pints.

PINEAPPLE JAM

*Keep pineapple sherbet in your freezer
to make a "double pineapple sundae"
using this delicious jam.*

2 ripe pineapples
Approximately 4 cups of sugar (2 pounds)
Juice of 4 lemons

Peel, core and chop the pineapples. Measure the pulp. (There should be about 4 cups.) Measure out 1 cup of sugar for each cup of pulp. Combine the pulp, sugar and lemon juice in a preserving kettle and cook uncovered over medium heat until sugar has dissolved, stirring frequently. Then cook over high heat for 30 minutes. Skim off the foam with a metal spoon, if needed. Ladle into hot, sterilized jars and seal immediately according to directions in Chapter 1.
Makes about 8 half-pints.

PINEAPPLE AND APRICOT JAM

2-1/2 pounds of apricots
3 cups of crushed pineapple (canned may be used)
Juice of 1 lemon
5 cups of sugar (2-1/2 pounds)

Wash and pit apricots. Cut into large pieces. Mix apricots, crushed pineapple with its juice, lemon juice and sugar together in a preserving kettle and cook over medium heat until sugar has dissolved, stirring frequently. Then cook over high heat for about 30 minutes, stirring frequently. Skim off foam with a metal spoon, if needed. Ladle into hot, sterilized jars and seal immediately according to directions in Chapter 1.
Makes approximately 11 half-pints.

Jams

RASPBERRY JAM

2 pounds of raspberries
3 cups of sugar (1-1/2 pounds)
Juice of 1 lemon

Wash and mash raspberries. Put into a preserving kettle and add sugar. Bring slowly to a boil, stirring until sugar has dissolved. Cook rapidly uncovered for about 25 to 30 minutes, or until thick, stirring frequently from the bottom to prevent sticking. Add lemon juice a few minutes before cooking is complete. Skim off foam with a metal spoon, if needed. Pour into hot, sterilized jars and seal immediately as directed in Chapter 1.
Makes approximately 5 half-pints.

RASPBERRY AND BLACK CHERRY JAM

1-1/2 pounds of black cherries
1 pound of raspberries
4 cups of sugar (2 pounds)

Wash and pit cherries. Put them into a preserving kettle and cook uncovered until tender, about 15 minutes. Wash the raspberries and crush them with the sugar. Add to the preserving kettle. Simmer until sugar has dissolved, stirring frequently. Then cook the mixture, uncovered, over high heat about 35 minutes, stirring more frequently toward the end of cooking time. Skim off foam with a metal spoon, if needed. Ladle into hot, sterilized jars and seal immediately according to directions in Chapter 1.
Makes approximately 4 half-pints.

RHUBARB-ORANGE JAM

Another tea-time treat!

4 pounds of rhubarb
8 cups of sugar (4 pounds)
2 tablespoons of freshly grated orange rind
1-1/2 cups of freshly squeezed orange juice
1/2 teaspoon of ground nutmeg
1 teaspoon of ground allspice

Wash the rhubarb and cut into 1-inch pieces. (Peel the rhubarb only if the skin is not tender.) Place in a preserving kettle. Add the sugar, cover and let stand overnight. In the morning, add the orange rind and juice, nutmeg and allspice and bring slowly to a boil over high heat, stirring frequently. Boil for about 35 minutes. Skim off foam with a metal spoon, if needed. Ladle into hot, sterilized jars and seal immediately according to directions in Chapter 1.
Makes approximately 10 half-pints.

STRAWBERRY JAM

2-1/2 pounds of strawberries
6 cups of sugar (3 pounds)
Juice of 1 lemon

Wash, drain, hull and crush the strawberries. Put strawberries into a preserving kettle and add sugar and lemon juice. Cook slowly, stirring occasionally, until sugar has dissolved. Now cook rapidly until thick, about 30 minutes. As mixture thickens, stir frequently from the bottom to prevent sticking. Skim off foam with a metal spoon, if needed. Ladle into hot, sterilized jars and seal immediately according to directions in Chapter 1. Makes approximately 6 half-pints.

Jams

STRAWBERRY-RHUBARB JAM

2 pounds of rhubarb
2 pounds of strawberries
7 cups of sugar (3-1/2 pounds)

Wash and cut rhubarb into small pieces; leave the skin on if it is tender and pink. Put rhubarb into a bowl, sprinkle the sugar over it, cover and let stand in a cool place overnight. The next morning, place the rhubarb mixture into a preserving kettle. Wash, hull and dry the strawberries and add to the rhubarb. Bring quickly to a boil and boil about 25 minutes, or until thick. Remove from heat and skim off foam with a metal spoon. Ladle into hot, sterilized jars and seal immediately according to directions in Chapter 1.
Makes approximately 9 half-pints.

OLD-FASHIONED SUNSHINE STRAWBERRY JAM

You need a very hot, still day to do this.

1-1/2 pounds of ripe strawberries
4 cups of sugar (2 pounds)
Juice of 1 lemon

Wash and hull strawberries. Put into a preserving kettle with sugar and lemon juice and heat slowly to boiling point. Cook rapidly about 10 minutes. Pour berry mixture into 1/2-inch-deep platters or shallow containers. Cover with a sheet of glass or saran wrap, propping the cover up to leave about 1 to 2 inches between it and the pan to allow for evaporation. Set outside in the sun. As the fruit cooks in the sun, turn it with a spatula 2 or 3 times during the day. If the sun is not hot enough, or a wind comes up during the day, the jam can take 2 or 3 days before it is ready. When it has thickened enough, pour into hot, sterilized jars and seal according to directions in Chapter 1.
Makes approximately 4 half-pints.

STRAWBERRY JAM WITH PECTIN

*Fill your pantry with these
as this is the jam everyone loves.*

2-1/2 pounds of fully ripe strawberries
1/4 cup of powdered pectin
7 cups of sugar (3-1/2 pounds)

Wash and hull the strawberries. Crush berries a layer at a time so they are reduced to a pulp. Put them in a preserving kettle with the pectin and mix thoroughly. Place over high heat and stir until mixture comes to a hard boil. Immediately add sugar and bring slowly to a full rolling boil, stirring frequently. Boil hard 1 minute, stirring constantly. Remove from stove and skim off foam with a metal spoon. Skim and stir for 5 minutes to prevent fruit from floating. Ladle into hot, sterilized jars and seal immediately according to directions in Chapter 1.
Makes approximately 8 half-pints.

Jams

RED TOMATO JAM

2-1/4 pounds of tomatoes
Juice of 2 lemons
1-1/2 teaspoons of freshly grated lemon rind
1/4 cup of powdered pectin
4-1/2 cups of sugar (2-1/4 pounds)

Blanch, peel and chop the tomatoes. Simmer them, uncovered, in a preserving kettle for 10 minutes. Add the lemon juice and rind and pectin to the preserving kettle, mixing thoroughly. Place over high heat and bring to a hard boil. Immediately add the sugar, stir in well and bring slowly to a full rolling boil. Boil hard for 1 minute, stirring constantly. Remove from heat and skim off foam with a metal spoon. Ladle into hot, sterilized jars and seal immediately according to directions in Chapter 1.
Makes approximately 5 half-pints.

WATERMELON JAM

*This recipe may be doubled
if your watermelon is large.*

1 3-pound watermelon
3 cups of sugar (1-1/2 pounds)

Peel and seed the watermelon; dice the flesh. Put 1 layer of watermelon into a bowl and add a layer of sugar; continue until all of the watermelon and sugar have been used. Cover the bowl and let it stand in a cool place for 4 hours. Place this mixture in a preserving kettle and cook over moderate heat, stirring frequently, until mixture is thick, about 45 to 50 minutes. Skim off foam with a metal spoon, if needed. Ladle into hot, sterilized jars and seal immediately according to directions in Chapter 1. Makes approximately 4 half-pints.

Apples and the National Debt

AMELIA SIMMONS in her *American Cookery* spoke of the irresistible pull of the apple orchard for small boys and the havoc they inflict. She seems insensitive to the joy of climbing an apple tree, straddling a limb and plucking and eating a peck of ripe apples on a summer afternoon. Lads who impatiently attack the green apples court a back-bending stomachache and attendant maladies. But Ms. Simmons makes a point, which was certainly applicable when her book was published in 1796. She argues that the apple tree can grow in almost any neglected corner of the family lot. If a boy were to plant an apple tree in an unused part of the yard, tend to it properly, and fend off the raids of his feckless companions, millions of trees would spring into growth at a great savings to the nation. Ms. Simmons maintains that the savings over a period of time would extinguish the national debt, while enriching the country's cookery. At the time she made the suggestion, her argument had merit. The public debt in 1796 was roughly $60 million.

Her scheme, however, would not work today. The apple harvest of 1974 was worth several times the national debt of 1796. Unfortunately, the U.S. debt in mid-1974 was $485 billion. If every boy in the country were to plant an apple tree and tend and guard it, there is no way the produce could cover our outstanding debt. We are a nation of apple eaters, but to ask us to eat $485 billion worth is a bit much.

Amelia Simmon's idea has merit even today, if we broaden its application. Plant fruits and vegetables in every unused corner of your yard, and by preserving and conserving, you can help drive down the high prices that send you reeling from the check-out counter.

VI Jellies

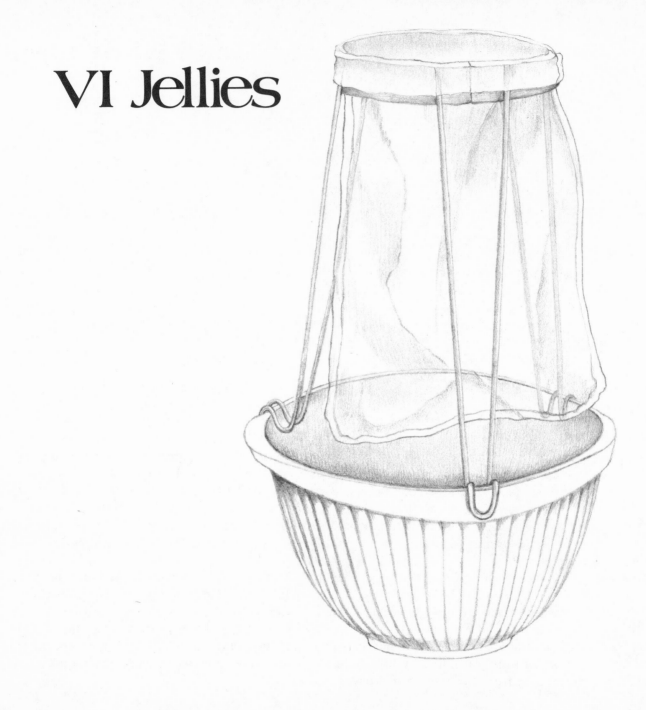

Ultra-Canal with Lafcadio Hearn

L AFCADIO HEARN was an exotic. When the World Industrial Exposition opened in New Orleans in December of 1884, he contributed a cookbook, *The Creole Cuisine,* with the understanding that his name not be used as author of the book. *The Creole Cuisine* has long since been identified as his creation. Like most of his work, it identifies with subjects foreign to the American temper. His interest was with the Creole, or Ultra-Canal, section of New Orleans, removed by a stretch of water from the brasher American part of the city. In his *Creole Sketches* he records the street cries of Ultra-Canal, modeled on the famous *Street Cries of London.* At dawn the peddlers emerged, chanting their singing commercials, "sung by Italians, negroes, Frenchmen and Spaniards." The fowl seller intones "Chick-EN, Madamma, Chicken-EN," to be followed by the seller of "Lem-ONS, fine Lem-ONS." In their wake come the purveyors of "Ap-PULLS" and "Straw-BARE-eries." The seller of cantaloupes had a song imitated by all of the children in the Creole quarter.

> Cantel-lope-ah!
> Fresh and fine,
> Jus from the vine,
> Only a dime.

Not all of the street vendors sold food. There was the Clothespole Man, whose cry could be heard from a great distance on a clear day. "Clo-ho-ho-ho-ho-ho-se-poles." And the merry Gascon "Coaly-coaly" man. The fig seller tended to slur his cries, so that "Fresh figs" became "Ice crags," and the fan vendor whose "Cheap fans" became "Jap-ans" or "Chapped hands." Returning to the vegetable kingdom, Hearn recalls the street cry of "TOM-ate-toes" and wonders, "Whose toes?"

The *Voices of Dawn,* as he entitled his street cries, appeared as a column in the New Orleans *Item.* It was the second paper in the city he had worked for, and later he moved on to the *Times-Democrat.* Meanwhile, his articles had received acceptance from *Century Magazine* and *Harper's Weekly.* Hearn had gone hungry in Cincinnati, his first true landfall in America. And he had gone hungry in New Orleans, between jobs at the *Commercial* and the *Item.* His vivid and perceptive articles in the Eastern magazines were to erase the specter of hunger from his life. *Harper's* commissioned him to write a series of articles on the West Indies, and he spent two years touring the islands. His longest stay was in the town of Saint-Pierre on Martinique. His attachment to the town and to the island was such he vowed never to leave. Fortunately, financial pressures forced him to in 1889. Five years later, Mont Pelée, which towered over the city, erupted in one of the most destructive volcanoes in modern times, and of the 20,000 citizens of Saint-Pierre only one survived, a prisoner deep in a dungeon.

Hearn had been born in Greece of a British Army surgeon and a Greek mother. At an early age he had been sent to relatives in Ireland and attended St. Cuthbert's School where he had lost an eye in a schoolboy game. His interest in literature and his reading habits soon strained the sound eye, and it grew bulbous, so that Hearn considered himself a "cyclops." He was preternaturally shy, because of his imagined grotesque appearance. Yet he made firm and influential friends, in and outside of literary circles.

He was shipped to the United States by an aunt, who had tired of his aversion to formal schooling. Arriving with very few dollars and no friends, he made his way to Cincinnati, where he entered a career in journalism after a short tenure as an assistant librarian. He became enamored of a mulatto woman who had befriended him, and tried to marry her, but was blocked by a state law against miscegenation. His colorful writing for the Cincinnati *Enquirer* caught the attention of the publisher of the New Orleans *Commercial,* and led to the job offer which brought him to the Crescent City.

Lafcadio Hearn is chiefly known for his books on Japan. *Harper's Weekly* commissioned him to do a series of articles on that country, and he sailed in the spring of 1890, intending to return in a year or two. It was not to be; shortly after arriving in Japan he severed his relationship with *Harper's* in a dispute over money. Once again Hearn was faced with privation. Luckily he met Captain Mitchell McDonald, a paymaster of the United States Navy in Yokohama, who had read Hearn's work and recognized his ability. He tided Hearn over the trying months, and secured him a position as a teacher in Satsue, in western Japan. Here Hearn met and married the daughter of a distinguished Japanese family, Setsuko Koizumi, who bore him a son. Then began the happiest years of the author's life. This was was also the most prolific period of Hearn's life, as book followed book: *Glimpses of Unfamiliar Japan, Kokoro, Gleanings in Buddha-Fields, Exotics and Retrospectives, In Ghostly Japan, Kwaidan, Japan: An Attempt at Interpretation.* The last book is of greatest interest to the student of Japanese history. Hearn's affinity was to the old Japan; the new Japan that he saw emerging after the arrival of Commodore Perry's "black ships" filled him with foreboding. He foretold the coming of an aggressive, expansionist, militaristic Japan, opposed to the quaint, hermetic island he had first known and loved. In his last years, Hearn earned his living by teaching at the Imperial University in Tokyo. One day an English traveler intruded on his class, and asked if Hearn would not mind his sitting in on a lecture. Lafcadio did mind, and he stormed out of the class, never to return to the university.

Hearn's Japanese works were the crown of his career, but his literary reputation was established in New Orleans. His unsigned *Creole Cuisine* has been followed by many Creole cookbooks, and preceded by a few. For a man no more attached to the kitchen than he, it was a triumph.

BLACKBERRY JELLY

*This is especially good
with English muffins and cream cheese.*

6 pounds of blackberries
1/4 cup of powdered pectin
4-1/2 cups of sugar (2-1/4 pounds)

Wash the berries in cold running water; do not let fruit stand in water. Simmer uncovered for about 10 minutes to extract the juice, stirring occasionally. Put fruit through a jelly bag to extract juice. Measure juice into a preserving kettle; there should be 3-1/2 cups. If there is less than 3-1/2 cups, add enough water to make this amount. Add the pectin and stir thoroughly. Place on high heat, stirring constantly, and bring quickly to a full rolling boil that cannot be stirred down. Add the sugar, continue stirring and heat again slowly to a full rolling boil. Boil hard for 1 minute. Remove from heat and skim off foam quickly with a metal spoon. Pour jelly into hot, sterilized jars and seal immediately according to directions in Chapter 1.
Makes approximately 6 half-pints.

CHERRY JELLY

3 pounds of fully ripe Morello cherries
1/2 cup of water
1/4 cup of powdered pectin
4-1/2 cups of sugar (2-1/4 pounds)

Wash, stem and pit cherries. Crush with potato masher, add 1/2 cup of water and simmer covered in a preserving kettle about 15 minutes. Place fruit in a jelly bag and extract juice. There should be about 3-1/2 cups; if juice is slightly less, add water to make this amount. Mix powdered pectin with juice in a preserving kettle. Bring quickly to a hard boil, stirring occasionally. Immediately add sugar and cook over medium heat, stirring frequently, until sugar has dissolved. Bring to a full rolling boil that cannot be stirred down and boil hard for 1 minute. Remove from heat and skim off foam with a metal spoon. Pour at once into hot, sterilized jars and seal immediately according to directions in Chapter 1.
Makes approximately 5 half-pints.

Jellies

CRANBERRY JELLY

This is great with second-day turkey.

1 pound of cranberries
2 cups of water
2 cups of sugar (1 pound)

In a preserving kettle, boil cranberries and water, covered, for about 10 minutes, or until the berries pop. Force cranberries through a sieve or a ricer (a sieve, 8 inches in diameter, will hold these). Add the sugar and stir and simmer until the sugar has dissolved. Then boil 10 minutes. Remove from heat and skim off the foam with a metal spoon. Ladle into hot, sterilized jars and seal immediately according to directions in Chapter 1.
Makes approximately 4 half-pints.

CRAB APPLE JELLY

3 pounds of crab apples
3 cups of water
Approximately 5 cups of sugar (2-1/2 pounds)

Select firm, sound crab apples. Wash and remove stems and blossoms. Cut fruit into halves, but do not core or peel. Place them into a preserving kettle, add the water, and bring to a boil on high heat. Reduce heat and simmer for 20 minutes, covered, until crab apples are soft. Strain fruit through a jelly bag. Measure juice; you should have about 6 cups. Cook the juice in batches of 3 to 4 cups at a time. For each cup of juice, measure 3/4 cup of sugar and set aside. Boil juice rapidly for about 5 minutes. Now add sugar, stirring constantly until it dissolves, and boil rapidly again. After 5 minutes, start test for jelly. Place a small amount of jelly in a spoon, cool slightly and let it drop back into kettle from the side of the spoon. As the syrup thickens, 2 large drops will form along the edge of the spoon, 1 on either side. When the 2 drops come together and fall as 1 drop, it is at sheeting stage, or 220° to 222° on a jelly thermometer. Remove from heat and ladle into hot, sterilized jars and seal immediately according to directions in Chapter 1.
Makes approximately 5 half-pints.

RED CURRANT JELLY

This is a must with roast beef or chicken.

5 pounds of red currants
Approximately 3-3/4 cups of sugar (1-7/8 pounds)

Wash the currants and pick them over. Place them in a preserving kettle, cover and bring slowly to a boil. Boil for 10 minutes, stirring occasionally. Strain the currants through a jelly bag. Measure the juice into the kettle and add 3/4 cup of sugar for each cup of juice. Bring slowly to a boil until sugar dissolves. Then boil for about 20 minutes, stirring from time to time until the jelly thermometer reads 220° to 222°, or the mixture sheets when dropped from a spoon (2 drops come together and fall as 1 drop). Remove from heat and skim with a metal spoon. Ladle into hot, sterilized jars and seal immediately according to directions in Chapter 1. Makes approximately 5 half-pints.

Jellies

ELDERBERRY JELLY

A nice, dry jelly for rich meats.

3 pounds of ripe elderberries
Juice of 2 lemons
1/4 cup of powdered pectin
4-1/2 cups of sugar (2-1/4 pounds)

Wash elderberries, remove larger stems and crush. Heat berries slowly in a preserving kettle until the juice starts to flow. Now cover and simmer about 20 minutes. Remove from heat, place in a jelly bag and extract the juice. Measure the juice; if there are less than 4-1/2 cups, make it up with water. Mix berry juice, lemon juice and powdered pectin and bring to a hard boil. Boil hard for 1 minute, stirring occasionally. Add sugar at once, stirring in well until it has dissolved. Bring to a full rolling boil. Boil hard again for 1 minute, stirring constantly. Remove from the stove and skim off foam with a metal spoon. Ladle into hot, sterilized jars and seal immediately according to directions in Chapter 1.
Makes approximately 4 half-pints.

GOOSEBERRY JELLY

Wonderful with Cornish hens!

4 pounds of gooseberries
Approximately 10 cups of sugar (5 pounds)

Wash the berries and place in a preserving kettle with barely enough water to cover them. Simmer gently, covered, until they are completely tender. Strain through a jelly bag. Measure the juice and add 1 cup of sugar for each cup of extracted juice. Return to the heat and stir until all the sugar is dissolved. Then boil rapidly until the jelly thermometer registers 220° to 222°, or the jelly sheets (2 drops coming together and forming 1 large drop) when dropped from a spoon. Ladle into hot, sterilized jars and seal immediately according to directions in Chapter 1.
Makes approximately 14 half-pints.

CONCORD GRAPE JELLY

3-1/2 pounds of ripe Concord grapes
1/2 cup of water
7 cups of sugar (3-1/2 pounds)
1/2 bottle of liquid pectin (3 ounces)

Wash and stem grapes; crush and put them in a preserving kettle. Cover and bring to a boil over high heat; reduce the heat and simmer for 10 minutes. Place fruit in a jelly bag and let drip to extract the juice. Cover the juice and let it stand in a cool place overnight. The next morning, strain through 2 thicknesses of damp cheesecloth to remove crystals. Measure 4 cups of juice into a preserving kettle; if you are short on juice, add water to make this amount. Stir in the sugar, and over medium heat, stir until sugar dissolves. Place over high heat and bring to a full rolling boil, stirring constantly. Add the pectin and bring again to a full rolling boil. Boil hard for 1 minute. Remove from heat and skim with a metal spoon. Quickly ladle into hot, sterilized jars and seal immediately according to directions in Chapter 1.
Makes approximately 8 half-pints.

GRAPE JELLY

4 pounds of slightly underripe Concord grapes
2/3 cup of water
Approximately 6 cups of sugar (3 pounds)

Wash and remove stems from grapes and put into a preserving kettle; add the water. Heat to boiling, then simmer covered for about 10 minutes. Place fruit in a jelly bag to extract the juice. Measure juice into a preserving kettle. Measure 3/4 cup of sugar for each cup of juice and set aside. Cook juice at a rapid boil for about 4 minutes. Add sugar, stirring until sugar has dissolved, and boil rapidly again. Test for jellying point about 5 minutes after sugar has been added by using a jelly thermometer which should read 220° to 222°, or by dipping a spoon into the mixture to see if the syrup sheets from the spoon (2 drops forming on the edge of the spoon, coming together and falling as 1 drop). Ladle into hot, sterilized jars and seal immediately according to directions in Chapter 1. Makes approximately 6 half-pints.

Jellies

GUAVA JELLY

This is good with cold meats or fowl.

2 pounds of guavas
2-1/4 cups of water
1/2 cup of freshly squeezed lemon juice
7 cups of sugar (3-1/2 pounds)
1/2 bottle of liquid pectin (3 ounces)

Wash, trim and slice the guavas. In a preserving kettle, combine guavas with the water and cook until they are soft. Mash this mixture thoroughly. Put into a jelly bag and extract the juice without squeezing. Measure out 3-1/2 cups of berry juice; if you are short on juice, add water to make 3-1/2 cups. Combine with the lemon juice and sugar in a preserving kettle and mix thoroughly. Place over high heat and bring slowly to a full rolling boil, stirring constantly. Immediately pour in pectin and stir. Bring mixture back to a rolling boil and boil hard for 1 minute. While still stirring, remove from the stove and skim off the foam with a metal spoon. Pour into hot, sterilized jars and seal immediately according to directions in Chapter 1.
Makes approximately 8 half-pints.

LEMON MINT JELLY

Melt and pour over chocolate ice cream for a mint sundae.

1-1/2 cups of fresh mint leaves (firmly packed)
2-1/4 cups of water
Approximately 3-1/2 cups of sugar (1-3/4 pounds)
3/4 cup of freshly squeezed lemon juice
1/2 bottle of liquid pectin (3 ounces)
Green food coloring

Wash mint leaves and stems; put them into a preserving kettle and crush with a potato masher to extract the oils. Add water and bring to a boil; remove from heat and let stand, covered, for about 20 minutes before straining. Measure juice into preserving kettle; add an equal amount of sugar. Add lemon juice, place over high heat and bring slowly to a boil, stirring constantly. Add liquid pectin at once; then bring to a full rolling boil and boil hard 1 minute, stirring constantly. Remove from heat, add a few drops of green food coloring and skim off foam with a metal spoon. Ladle into hot, sterilized jars and seal immediately according to directions in Chapter 1.
Makes approximately 3 half-pints.

POMEGRANATE JELLY

12 fully ripe pomegranates
7-1/2 cups of sugar (3-3/4 pounds)
1 6-ounce bottle of liquid pectin

    Cut the pomegranates in half and extract the juice with an orange squeezer. Place the juice in a jelly bag and squeeze it through. Measure 4 cups of juice into a preserving kettle; add water if needed to bring juice to 4 cups. Add the sugar and bring slowly to a boil over high heat, stirring constantly. Add the liquid pectin and bring the jelly again to a full rolling boil that cannot be stirred down. Boil hard for 1 minute. Remove from the heat and skim with a metal spoon. Ladle into hot, sterilized jars and seal immediately according to directions in Chapter 1.
Makes approximately 8 half-pints.

Jellies

PEACH AND PLUM JELLY

2 pounds of ripe peaches
1 pound of ripe plums
3/4 cup of water
4 cups of sugar (2 pounds)
1/4 cup of powdered pectin

Wash peaches and plums; cut coarsely without bothering to pit or peel. Put them into a preserving kettle with the water and bring to a boil. Simmer, covered, for 15 minutes. Place fruit in a jelly bag and strain off juice. Measure 3 cups of juice; if there is not quite enough juice, add a little water to the pulp in the jelly bag and strain once more. Add to juice to make 3 cups. In preserving kettle, combine the juice, sugar and powdered pectin and stir thoroughly. Place over high heat and bring the mixture slowly to a boil. Boil for 1 minute, stirring constantly. Remove from heat and skim with a metal spoon. Ladle into hot, sterilized jars and seal immediately according to directions in Chapter 1. Makes approximately 5 half-pints.

PEACH JELLY

Heavenly on hot scones.

3 pounds of firm ripe peaches
1-3/4 cups of water
1/4 cup of freshly squeezed lemon juice
4-1/2 cups of sugar (2-1/4 pounds)
1/4 cup of powdered pectin

Wash, blanch, peel and pit the peaches. Place them in a preserving kettle and mash thoroughly. Add the water and lemon juice to the pulp and simmer, covered, for 10 minutes. Extract the juice through a jelly bag. Measure the juice into a preserving kettle; if there are less than 3-1/2 cups, add water to bring the juice to this amount. Add the pectin and mix thoroughly. Place the juice on high heat and bring it to a boil, stirring continually. Add the sugar and mix well until sugar has dissolved. Bring this again to a full rolling boil that cannot be stirred down. Boil for exactly 2 minutes. Remove from heat and skim with a metal spoon. Ladle into hot, sterilized jars and seal immediately according to directions in Chapter 1.
Makes approximately 6 half-pints.

RED PEPPER JELLY

One glass of this with one glass
of green-chili pepper jelly would make
a decorative Christmas present.

2-1/2 pounds of sweet red peppers (about
    7 large peppers)
2 cups of cider vinegar
2 teaspoons of salt
2 teaspoons of chili powder
10 cups of sugar (5 pounds)
2/3 cup of freshly squeezed lemon juice
1 6-ounce bottle of liquid pectin

Wash and cut up peppers, discarding seeds. Put a few at a time into a blender until finely chopped (should make about 4 cups). In a preserving kettle, combine chopped peppers, vinegar, salt and chili powder. Over high heat, bring to a boil and boil for 10 minutes. Remove from the heat and add sugar and lemon juice, mixing well. Return to the heat and bring slowly to a full boil. Stir in the pectin and bring again to a hard boil, stirring constantly, for exactly 1 minute. Remove from the stove and skim off foam with a metal spoon. Ladle into hot, sterilized jars and seal immediately according to directions in Chapter 1.
Makes about 14 half-pints.

GREEN CHILI-PEPPER JELLY

2 long green chili peppers (about 4 inches)
1 medium-size green bell pepper
1-1/2 cups of cider vinegar
5 cups of sugar (2-1/2 pounds)
1 teaspoon of cayenne pepper
1/2 teaspoon of green food coloring
1/2 bottle of liquid pectin (3 ounces)

Wash, seed and chop the chilies and bell pepper. In a blender, put 1/2 cup of the vinegar; add chilies and bell pepper and liquify. In a preserving kettle, mix sugar, cayenne pepper and peppers. Use remaining cup of vinegar to rinse blender and add to the mixture. Bring slowly to a boil, stirring constantly. Boil 2 minutes. Remove from heat, skim foam with a metal spoon and add green food coloring. Stir in pectin and mix well. Ladle into hot, sterilized jars and seal immediately according to directions in Chapter 1.
Makes approximately 5 half-pints.

Jellies

QUINCE JELLY

3-1/2 pounds of quinces
7 cups of water
1/4 cup of freshly squeezed lemon juice
3 cups of sugar (1-1/2 pounds)

Wash and remove stems and blossoms from quinces, but do not peel or core. Slice the quinces very thin and place them in a preserving kettle. Add the water, cover and bring to a boil over high heat. Reduce heat and simmer for 25 minutes. Extract the juice by dripping it through a jelly bag. Return the juice to the heat and add lemon juice and sugar, mixing well. Bring slowly to a boil over high heat until the jelly thermometer measures 220° to 222°, or until the jelly mixture sheets (2 drops come together and fall as 1 drop) when dropped from a spoon. Skim off the foam quickly and ladle into hot, sterilized jars and seal immediately according to directions in Chapter 1.
Makes approximately 4 half-pints.

BLACK RASPBERRY JELLY

*This is truly a rare treat
as black raspberries are uncommon.*

6 pounds of black raspberries
7 cups of sugar (3-1/2 pounds)
1 tablespoon of freshly squeezed lemon juice
1 6-ounce bottle of liquid pectin

Wash raspberries in running water and crush them thoroughly; then simmer covered for 10 minutes. Put the fruit in a jelly bag and extract all juice possible. Measure 4 cups of juice. If there is less than 4 cups, add water to make this measure. Place raspberry juice, sugar and lemon juice in a preserving kettle and cook over high heat until it boils, stirring constantly. Immediately stir in the pectin. Then bring to a full rolling boil and boil hard for 1 minute, stirring constantly. Remove from heat and skim off foam with a metal spoon. Ladle into hot, sterilized jars and seal immediately according to directions in Chapter 1.
Makes approximately 10 half-pints.

STRAWBERRY JELLY

This is for steaming-hot biscuits.

4 pounds of fully ripe strawberries
7-1/2 cups of sugar (3-3/4 pounds)
1 6-ounce bottle of liquid pectin

Sort, wash and hull berries. In a large bowl, crush the berries 1 cup at a time so that all the juice is extracted and each berry is reduced to a pulp; strain through a jelly bag. Measure the juice into a preserving kettle; if there are less than 4 cups, add water to bring the juice to this amount. Place over heat, add the sugar and stir until sugar dissolves. Place on high heat and bring sugar and berries to a full rolling boil that cannot be stirred down. Add the liquid pectin and bring the jelly again to a full rolling boil. Boil hard for 1 minute. Remove from the heat and skim with a metal spoon. Ladle into hot, sterilized jars and seal immediately according to directions in Chapter 1.
Makes approximately 8 half-pints.

EUNICE'S WINE JELLY

Serve as highbrow dessert with whipped cream.

3 cups of sugar (1-1/2 pounds)
Grated rind of 1 lemon
2 cups of port (Muscatel or Tokay will do)
1/2 bottle of liquid pectin (3 ounces)

Heat water in the bottom of a double boiler until boiling. In the top, mix sugar, lemon rind and wine, stirring until sugar has dissolved. Stir constantly for 2 minutes. Add liquid pectin and stir in well. Pour into hot, sterilized jars and seal immediately according to directions in Chapter 1.
Makes approximately 4 half-pints.

The Orange Girl

I**T IS ONE** of history's ironies that Charles II of England should have taken for his queen a princess of the Portuguese house of Braganza. Portugal was England's principal source of oranges, and it was an orange seller who was to become one of the most celebrated royal mistresses in the long chronicle of the throne. Her name was Nell Gwyn, low born in a mean section of London known as the Coal Yard. Though little is known of her early life, by age 11 she is portrayed as wandering the cobbles of London hawking "fresh herring even ten a groat." In a year or two she came under the tutelage of Madame Ross, proprietor of a brothel in Lewknor Lane where Nell was employed as a serving girl. The establishment was frequented by London's rakes, and it is here that Nell may have acquired the salty vocabulary worthy of a drover, which was to mark her speech in the years that followed.

The Puritan Revolution had closed all the theaters. When Charles II was restored to the throne in 1660, plans were quickly drawn up for the construction of two theaters, one of them the King's Theater in Drury Lane. Nell gave up her herrings for oranges, and became one of the orange girls in the Drury Lane Theater. The girls, each bearing a basket of vine-covered oranges, formed a line across the pit, with their backs to the stage. They sold their fruit, as well as their favors, to gentlemen playgoers. The orange girls also acted as go-betweens, carrying messages, along with their fruit, from gentlemen to ladies in the audience. The girls were ruled by a strong-willed doxy known as Orange Moll.

It is doubtful that Charles II ever knew Nell as an orange girl, although he occasionally attended the theater. It was after the brash and gifted Nell had graduated from the pit to the stage that she attracted the royal eye. Her first leading performance was in *The Indian Emperor* by John Dryden. Her success was brief; the Great Plague descended on London a few weeks later and the theaters were forced to close. In the train of the plague (1665) came the Great Fire of London (1666), in which five-sixths of the city burned down. So the reopening of the theaters was further delayed. Nell's first appearance after theaters reopened is believed to have been in *The English Monsieur* by James Howard, a comedy in which she was much more at ease and in her element than in some of the heavier roles she played. Samuel Pepys loved her in comic roles, thought her miscast in tragedy.

Secret Love is thought to be the first play in which Charles II saw Nelly on the stage. He was charmed, and soon was meeting her at houses of assignation. The inevitable happened; on May 8, 1670, she bore him a son, one of a series of illegitimate sons Charles sired, though at his death he was left without a legitimate heir. Not too many months elapsed before Charles moved Nell into a house in Pall Mall, where he was a frequent visitor, and she bore him a second son.

Charles II was incapable of being a one-woman man. While still enamored of Nell, he took up with Louise de Querouailles, who had come from France as part of a diplomatic mission led by his sister,

Henrietta of France. Louise soon bore him a son, and received permission from the French king to become a British subject. Charles bestowed upon her the title of Duchess of Portsmouth. Daniel Defoe wrote that Louise as Duchess bridled when a friend praised her rival Nell Gwyn for her wit and beauty and told how Nell delighted the king with her repartée and fine mien. "Yes, Madam," said the Duchess, "but anybody may know she's an orange wench by her swearing."

Nell was to get a measure of revenge a few years later when Charles convened Parliament in Oxford, hoping for more cool deliberations in the ivy-towered university town. At the time, anti-French and anti-Papist feelings were running strong in England. When Nell drove into town in her gilded and spangled carriage, she was mistaken for the French-born Duchess of Portsmouth. A mob gathered around her coach, shouting imprecations and threats. She lowered the window and calmed the crowd down. "Be civil, good people, be civil. I am not she. I am the Protestant whore."

Meanwhile, the king had become entranced with yet another paramour, the beautiful Hortense Mancini, niece of Cardinal Mazarin. Charles lodged the Italian hard by St. James Palace. Of the half dozen or more women in his life, Hortense held the briefest tenure in his affections.

Nell Gwyn was as extravagant as she was sharp of tongue, a condition not helped by Charles' inclination to indulge her whims. He heaped upon her jewels and pounds and unlimited credit. Nell spent of her bounty at the card tables. Nor was that all Charles II had given her; he had given her Burford House close by Windsor Castle. Her second son was knighted the Duke of St. Albans and plans were advanced for granting darling Nell the title and perquisites of Countess of Greenwich, and all the pelf and equipage that went with it. It was not to be. As John Evelyn wrote of a Sabbath evening in his diary, "I can never forget the inexpressible luxury and profaneness, gaming and all dissoluteness, and as it were, total forgetfulness of God [it being a Sunday evening], which this day sennight I was witness of; the King sitting and toying with his concubines, Portsmouth [Louise], Cleveland [Katherine Villars], Mazarin [Hortense], etc., a French boy singing love-songs in that glorious gallery, whilst about twenty of the great courtiers and other dissolute persons were at basset [cards] round a large table, a bank of at least 2,000 pounds in gold before them; upon which two gentlemen who were with me made strange reflections. Six days after, all was in the dust."

Six days after Charles II was dead of apoplexy. Nell Gwyn's deep grief soon gave way to the fear of the debtors' jail as her creditors pressed in on her; she sold her jewelry, her silver plate, even boiled down her silver bedstead to keep them at bay. James II, Charles' successor, gave her succor in her distress. Nell herself was in ill health, and survived Charles by only two years. At age 37 she, too, died of apoplexy, an unlikely end for one so young. She was buried next to her mother in St. Martin's-in-the-Fields, laid to rest by Dr. Tenison, who was to become the Archbishop of Canterbury.

VII Marmalades

Diamond in the Rough

D IAMOND JIM BRADY was born to the amber, rather than the purple. He was born upstairs over his father's saloon on the lower West Side of Manhattan, and the drinks were on the house for the rest of the night. His father christened him James Buchanan Brady after the Democratic nominee for president in 1856. Diamond Jim was as big at birth as in later life—a squalling nine pounds. At an early age he foreswore the life as swamper at the saloon, for the calling of bellboy at the *de luxe* hotel St. James. It was here he struck up an acquaintance with an official of the New York Central, and through him was hired for a job in the baggage room of the railroad. The alert and forward young Irishman quickly ascended to the title of baggage master, and from then on his fortune was to be tied closely to the railroad business.

Diamond Jim had little more than a grade-school education, yet drudged away at Paine's night school to improve himself. At the time, he received a respectable salary of $50 a month, and spent much of it on clothes: the dress bespoke the man. He had become a regular theatergoer, using complimentary tickets which he got from merchants who posted playbills in their windows. These were not the front row center seats he was to command later in his career, when producers were to judge the success or failure of their shows by Diamond Jim's attention span. If he fell asleep in the first act, the show was a flop. If he stayed awake during the first two acts, the show had a good chance of success. If Jim remained awake through all three acts, the show was an unquestioned smash.

Through his friend at New York Central, Jim was hired by the railway supply house of Manning, Maxwell and Moore. The personable Diamond Jim soon became their best salesman. One of his first purchases before going on the road was a diamond ring; hotel clerks in those days tended to be snide toward a traveling man who did not sport a respectable diamond on his knuckle. In the case of James Buchanan Brady, as his fame and fortune grew, so did the number of diamonds that glittered from his hands, shirtfronts, lapels and cravats.

It may have been memories of his father's, later his stepfather's, saloon; in any event, Diamond Jim was a lifelong teetotaler. This bon vivant and one of the last of the big spenders never drank anything stronger than orange juice or root beer. The parties he gave were bacchanalian, and while his guests quaffed champagne or the finest of brandies, Jim quietly sipped his proofless drinks. It is to his credit that he never tried to sign a contract during the riotous evenings that sometimes ended after dawn. He always waited until the following day to present his proposition to his hung-over prospects. More often than not, they signed the contract Jim presented. It may have been the memory of the beautiful girls who had popped out of the oversized cakes and, naked as jaybirds, had sat in their laps; or it may have been remorse. Whatever the reason, the Brady system worked.

Jim Brady lived much of his time on an open-ended expense account. This accounting tool, which keeps most of the better bars and restaurants alive in the 1970's, was as sharp in the latter 19th and early 20th century as it is today. Nothing was too good for Brady's customers, or for Brady, and the bills submitted to the home office were often staggering; but so was the amount of business Jim wrote. The *maître d'* at Delmonico's, Rector's or the Waldorf popped to attention when Diamond Jim strolled in, often with an entourage that meant a successful evening. Jim's gustatory preference was for seafood, and his grand passion was for oysters and lobsters, especially oysters. George Rector had fresh oysters shipped up daily from Chesapeake Bay, and by his own account, every third barrel was marked "For Mr. Brady." Diamond Jim also had a sweet tooth, and a box of candies was a fixture on his desk. It is reliably reported that he was known to consume 20 pounds of candies on a weekend.

It is a mystery that Diamond Jim remained a bachelor all of his life, even allowing for the Irish tradition of choosing the single life over the plural. He knew and adored the most glamorous women of his epoch, including Lillian Russell and Lily Langtry. The one woman he truly loved was Edna McCauley, a girl content to be his mistress and share his lavish house at 86th Street. But marriage, no. Jim had bought a place in the country for relaxation, but the weekends there with Flo Ziegfeld, Anna Held, Lillian Russell and Jessie Lewisohn—the last an old partner in the deals that had brought wealth to Diamond Jim—were more taxing than relaxing. The consequences were devastating to Brady; Edna McCauley fell in love with Lewisohn, and shortly after they married. There is no evidence Diamond Jim seriously thought of matrimony afterward, except a half-hearted proposal to his old friend Lillian Russell, which she turned down.

James Buchanan Brady had progressed from super-salesman to financier. His friendship with John W. "Bet a Million" Gates had much to do with it. Gates was the avowed antagonist of J. Pierpont Morgan, and on at least two occasions—the sale of American Steel and Wire Company to newly organized United States Steel Corporation, and his corner of Louisville & National Railroad—he beat Morgan on his own turf. Meanwhile Jim, through shrewd investments in stocks and commodities, built his personal fortune to approximately $12 million, and his yearly income to roughly $1 million. In those pretax times, it was not as easy to spend this amount without working at it. Jim did. He gave a dinner at the Hoffman House which lasted from 4 p.m. Sunday until 9 a.m. Monday. The tab for the 50 guests came to $100,000. Diamond Jim was truly one of the last, if not the last, of the big spenders.

MILLIE'S CARROT MARMALADE

Surprisingly good!

1 pound of carrots
2 medium-size oranges
Juice of 4 medium-size lemons
7 cups of sugar (3-1/2 pounds)
1/2 bottle of liquid pectin (3 ounces)

   Wash and shred carrots and put them into a preserving kettle. Remove seeds from the oranges and put through a meat grinder or chop them. Add to the carrots with the lemon juice and sugar. Over high heat, bring the mixture slowly to a rapid boil. Boil for 5 minutes, stirring constantly. Remove from the heat and stir in the pectin. With a metal spoon, skim and stir for 5 minutes to prevent carrots from floating. Ladle into hot, sterilized jars and seal immediately according to directions in Chapter 1.
Makes approximately 6 half-pints.

CHERRY MARMALADE

An unusual marmalade for your favorite guests. George Washington may have made this from the fruit of his cherry tree, as it is a very old recipe.

3-1/2 pounds of cherries
3 cups of sugar (1-1/2 pounds)
2 cups of water
Juice and grated rind of 1 orange
Juice and grated rind of 1 lemon

   Wash, stem and pit the cherries. Combine them with sugar and water in a preserving kettle. Simmer the cherries, uncovered, for 15 minutes. Then add lemon and orange juice and grated rind. Bring to a boil again and boil for about 35 minutes until jelly thermometer reads 220° to 222°, or until syrup sheets when dropped from a spoon (2 drops coming together and falling as 1 drop). Skim with a metal spoon, stirring to keep fruit from floating. Ladle into hot, sterilized jars and seal immediately according to directions in Chapter 1.
Makes approximately 5 half-pints.

Marmalades

EGGPLANT MARMALADE

*This has a distinctive foreign flavor.
Make your guests bet on what it is!*

2 pounds of eggplant
4 cups of sugar (2 pounds)
4 cups of water
1 teaspoon of ground nutmeg
1-1/2 teaspoons of ground cinnamon
Juice of 2 large lemons
Grated rind of 1/2 lemon

Wash, peel and dice the eggplant. Barely cover with water in a preserving kettle and boil for about 10 minutes; drain and set aside. Make a syrup by combining the sugar, water, nutmeg and cinnamon and bringing them to a boil. Add the eggplant. Remove from heat, cover and allow to stand overnight. The next day, remove the eggplant with a slotted spoon and boil the syrup for 20 minutes to thicken it. Return the eggplant to the kettle and boil for 30 to 40 minutes until the syrup sheets when dropped from a spoon (2 drops forming on the edge of the spoon, coming together and falling as 1 drop), or until a jelly thermometer reads 200° to 222°. Stir in the lemon juice and grated rind. Ladle into hot, sterilized jars and seal according to directions in Chapter 1.
Makes approximately 8 half-pints.

WHITE FIG MARMALADE

A treat for your special house guests.

3 pounds of white figs
3 oranges
6-3/4 cups of sugar (3-3/8 pounds)
3 lemons

Wash, peel and chop the figs. Wash and chop the oranges, including the rind. Put figs and oranges in a preserving kettle with the sugar. Place on low heat and cook, uncovered, about 45 minutes, stirring occasionally. While this is simmering, wash, very thinly slice and seed the lemons. Cook them in a small amount of water until tender and drain. About 15 minutes before the fig mixture is done, add the lemon slices. Ladle into hot, sterilized jars and seal immediately according to directions in Chapter 1.
Makes approximately 9 half-pints.

GRAPE MARMALADE VERT

A lovely color for marmalade!

4 pounds of green Concord grapes
2 cups of water
8 cups of sugar (4 pounds)

Wash and seed grapes by halving them. Put grapes and the water into a preserving kettle and simmer uncovered until tender, about 20 minutes. Add sugar and bring slowly to a boil. Cook rapidly, stirring frequently, for about 30 minutes or until a jelly thermometer reads 220° to 222°, or syrup sheets when dropped from a spoon (2 drops coming together and falling as 1 drop). Ladle into hot, sterilized jars and seal immediately according to directions in Chapter 1.
Makes approximately 10 half-pints.

Marmalades

GRAPEFRUIT MARMALADE

2/3 cup of thinly sliced grapefruit peel
1-1/3 cups of chopped grapefruit pulp (about
   1 large grapefruit)
4 cups of water
Approximately 4 cups of sugar (2 pounds)

Cover grapefruit peel with water. Boil 10 minutes; then drain. Do this twice more to eliminate bitterness. When chopping the grapefruit pulp, be careful to eliminate all the white pith. Combine the chopped pulp, drained peel and 4 cups of water. Cover and let stand in the refrigerator for 12 to 18 hours. In a preserving kettle, cook the mixture rapidly until the peel is tender, about 40 minutes. Measure the fruit and liquid and add 1 cup of sugar for each cup of pulp to the kettle. Bring slowly to a boil, stirring frequently, until all the sugar has dissolved. Raise the heat and boil rapidly for 30 to 35 minutes, until a jelly thermometer reads 220° to 222°, or until the mixture sheets when dropped from a spoon (2 drops coming together to form 1 large drop). Stir frequently toward the end of cooking period to prevent sticking. Ladle into hot, sterilized jars and seal immediately according to directions in Chapter 1.
Makes approximately 4 half-pints.

CHUNKY GRAPEFRUIT MARMALADE

3 large grapefruits
3 lemons
6 cups of water
Approximately 6 cups of sugar (3 pounds)

Wash and place the whole grapefruits in a preserving kettle. Barely cover fruit with water and simmer slowly until tender. Remove from heat, cover and let grapefruits stand in the water overnight. Wash the lemons and thinly slice them, removing and reserving the seeds and the juice. Tie the seeds in a cheesecloth bag and put the lemon slices, lemon juice and cheesecloth bag in 6 cups of water; let stand overnight. The next morning, remove the grapefruits from their soaking water and discard the water. Cut grapefruits into chunks, putting the thick center pith and seeds into the cheesecloth bag with the lemon seeds. Put the grapefruit chunks, cheesecloth bag, lemon slices and their soaking water in a preserving kettle. Simmer uncovered until the peel is soft and half the liquid has evaporated, about 1 hour. Remove the cheesecloth bag and discard it. Measure the pulp and add 1 cup of sugar for each cup of pulp. Place kettle over medium heat and stir until sugar has dissolved. Then bring to a boil and boil rapidly until jelly thermometer reads 220° to 222°, or mixture sheets from a spoon (2 drops form, come together and fall as 1 drop). Remove kettle from heat and stir gently for 5 minutes to distribute the peel. Ladle into hot, sterilized jars and seal immediately according to directions in Chapter 1.
Makes approximately 12 half-pints.

LEMON SHRED MARMALADE

A tangy, eye-appealing treat;
very popular with the British.

5 lemons
1 grapefruit
12 cups of water
Approximately 8 cups of sugar (4 pounds)

Wash and peel the lemons thinly; remove the white pith and seeds and discard them. Cut the peel into fine shreds; reserve the pulp. Simmer the peel with 2 cups of the water in a covered preserving kettle for about 1 hour, or until tender. Drain the liquid from the lemon shreds and set both aside. Wash the grapefruit and cut it and the lemon pulp into small pieces; cover with the remaining 10 cups of water and simmer gently in a covered preserving kettle for 1-1/2 hours, or until the fruit is tender. Add the liquid from the lemon shreds to the kettle and bring just to a boil. Remove from heat and strain mixture through a jelly bag. Measure the juice into the preserving kettle and add 1 cup of sugar for each cup of juice. Add the reserved lemon shreds and over high heat, boil hard for about 15 minutes until a jelly thermometer reads 220° to 222°, or until mixture sheets from a spoon (2 drops come together and fall as 1 drop). Remove from heat and let stand for about 15 minutes; then stir gently to distribute the peel. Ladle into hot, sterilized jars and seal immediately according to directions in Chapter 1.
Makes approximately 10 half-pints.

RANGPUR LIME MARMALADE

12 small Rangpur limes
5 lemons
Approximately 4-1/2 cups of sugar (2-1/4 pounds)

Wash and remove the seeds of the limes and lemons and put fruits through a food chopper or cut in small pieces. Measure the pulp and add 3 cups of water for each cup of pulp; let stand overnight. The next morning, boil the mixture, uncovered, in a preserving kettle about 20 minutes. Remove mixture to a bowl, cover and let stand again overnight. The next morning, measure citrus mixture. Cooking batches of only 4 to 6 cups of fruit at a time, measure out 3/4 cup of sugar for each cup of fruit and combine fruit and sugar in a preserving kettle. Bring mixture slowly to a boil, stirring frequently until sugar has dissolved. Then boil rapidly for about 20 minutes until jellying point is reached. Test for jellying point with a jelly thermometer which should read 220°to 222°, or with a spoon which, when dipped into mixture, has 2 drops form along the edge, come together and fall as 1 drop. Ladle into hot, sterilized jars and seal immediately as directed in Chapter 1.
Makes approximately 6 half-pints.

Marmalades

LIME-PINE MARMALADE

A tangy spread for your breakfast.

1 grapefruit
2 limes
1 large pineapple
Approximately 5 cups of water
Approximately 5 cups of sugar (2-1/2 pounds)
2 tablespoons of freshly grated orange rind

Wash and remove the seeds of the limes and the grapefruit and dice or put them through a meat grinder. Pare, core and chop the pineapple. Measure all the fruit including the juice, and add 1-1/2 cups of water for each cup of fruit; let this stand overnight. The next morning, simmer the fruit and water, uncovered, over low heat until the fruit is tender, about 1 hour. Measure the mixture again and add the orange rind and 1 cup of sugar for each cup of pulp. Cook over medium heat until sugar has dissolved, stirring constantly. Then cook over high heat until your jelly thermometer reads 220° to 222°, or the syrup sheets (2 drops falling from the side of a spoon and forming 1 large drop). Ladle into hot, sterilized jars and seal immediately according to directions in Chapter 1.
Makes approximately 7 half-pints.

NECTARINE-ORANGE MARMALADE

A subtle sweet.

3 pounds of nectarines
3 medium-size oranges
4-1/2 cups of sugar (2-1/4 pounds)

Wash, blanch, peel and pit nectarines; wash the oranges. Remove the peel from 1-1/2 of the oranges and discard it. Put the nectarines and the peeled and unpeeled oranges through a meat grinder. There should be about 4-1/2 cups. Place the fruit in a preserving kettle, add 4-1/2 cups of sugar and bring slowly to a boil. Boil rapidly, uncovered, for about 30 minutes, stirring frequently. Skim off foam with a metal spoon. Ladle into hot, sterilized jars and seal immediately according to directions in Chapter 1.
Makes approximately 4 half-pints.

ORANGE MARMALADE

2 large oranges
2 lemons
5 cups of water
4 cups of sugar (2 pounds)

Wash and slice the fruit thinly. Remove the seeds and tie them in a cheesecloth bag. Put the fruit, water and cheesecloth bag into a preserving kettle and simmer uncovered for about 1-1/2 hours until the peel is soft. Remove the bag of seeds, squeezing it well to release all liquid. Add the sugar and, over medium heat, stir until it has dissolved. Bring to a boil and boil for about 10 minutes until a jelly thermometer reads 220° to 222°, or the mixture sheets when dropped from a spoon (2 drops coming together and falling as 1 drop). Remove from heat and stir gently for 5 minutes to distribute the peel. Ladle into hot, sterilized jars and seal immediately according to directions in Chapter 1.
Makes approximately 8 half-pints.

Marmalades

MANDARIN-PAPAYA MARMALADE

Lovely present for a shut-in.

2-1/2 pounds of tangerines
5 pounds of firm, ripe papayas
1 tablespoon of finely shredded fresh ginger root
Approximately 7-1/2 cups of sugar (3-3/4 pounds)

Wash the tangerines thoroughly; squeeze out all the juice and pulp and discard the seeds. Cut the tangerine rinds into thin strips with scissors and add them to the pulp and juice. Wash, peel, seed and chop the papaya and add the ginger to it. Combine these with the tangerine juice, rind and pulp and measure this mixture into a preserving kettle. There should be 7-1/2 cups; if there is more or less, adjust the amount of sugar to equal that of the pulp. Simmer, uncovered, until sugar has dissolved, stirring occasionally. Then boil this on a high heat for about 30 minutes, stirring frequently to keep from scorching. Skim and ladle into hot, sterilized jars and seal immediately according to directions in Chapter 1.
Makes approximately 10 half-pints.

PAPAYA AND GINGER MARMALADE

Delicious used as a filling for a jelly roll.

6 pounds of papayas
2 lemons
4 cups of water
2 teaspoons of finely chopped fresh ginger root
4 cups of sugar (2 pounds)
2 tablespoons of chopped preserved ginger

Wash, peel, seed and chop the papayas; this makes about 8 cups of fruit. Set aside. Wash, seed and slice lemons thinly; cut slices in half. Cook sliced lemon in 2 cups of the water until transparent. Now make a syrup by combining the fresh ginger and sugar with remaining 2 cups of water in a preserving kettle. Boil for 5 minutes. Add the syrup, preserved ginger and papaya to the lemons in the kettle and boil all the ingredients, uncovered, about 45 minutes, stirring frequently. Ladle into hot, sterilized jars and seal immediately according to directions in Chapter 1.
Makes approximately 12 half-pints.

GINGER-PEAR MARMALADE

A delightful tangy marmalade.

6 pounds of pears
2 cups of sweet cider
1 6-ounce jar of preserved ginger
8 cups of sugar (4 pounds)
Juice of 1 lemon

Wash the pears and dice them. Do not peel or core them. Heat the cider in a preserving kettle; add the pears and simmer gently until they are tender, about 20 minutes. Put them through a sieve and return to the preserving kettle. Finely chop the ginger and add it, along with the sugar and lemon juice, to the kettle. Bring slowly to a boil, stirring until the sugar has dissolved, about 15 minutes. Then boil quickly, stirring constantly, about 25 minutes until the jelly thermometer reads 220° to 222°, or until the syrup sheets (2 drops coming together and falling as 1 drop) when dropped from a spoon. Ladle into hot, sterilized jars and seal immediately according to directions in Chapter 1. Makes approximately 11 half-pints.

SPICED PRUNE MARMALADE

2 pounds of dried pitted prunes
3 cups of sugar (1-1/2 pounds)
1 cup of cider vinegar
1 teaspoon of ground cloves
1 teaspoon of ground cinnamon

Soak the prunes overnight in water to cover. The next morning, simmer in the same water until they are tender. Remove prunes from water and cut into pieces; reserve soaking water. Put prunes in a preserving kettle with the reserved liquid and add sugar, vinegar and spices. Simmer this mixture uncovered until thick, about 40 minutes. Ladle into hot, sterilized jars and seal immediately according to directions in Chapter 1.
Makes approximately 4 half-pints.

Marmalades

RHUBARB MARMALADE

4 pounds of rhubarb
6 oranges
1 lemon
6 cups of sugar (3 pounds)

Wash rhubarb, oranges and lemon and put with peel through a meat grinder, or dice them. Combine fruit and sugar in a preserving kettle and bring slowly to a boil. Cook the marmalade uncovered over high heat for about 20 to 30 minutes until it sheets when dropped from a spoon (2 drops coming together and falling as 1 drop), or until it measures 220° to 222° on a jelly thermometer. Ladle into hot, sterilized jars and seal immediately according to directions in Chapter 1.
Makes approximately 14 half-pints.

WATERMELON MARMALADE

6 cups of chopped watermelon rind
6 cups of water
6-1/2 cups of sugar (3-1/4 pounds)
1/4 cup of freshly grated orange rind
1 cup of freshly squeezed orange juice
Juice of 2 lemons
Juice of 1 lime

Trim the green skin and pink pulp from the thick watermelon rind. Chop rind and measure out 6 cups; then soak the chopped rind in the water for 18 hours. In a preserving kettle, combine rind, soaking water and all remaining ingredients. Cook over low heat, stirring frequently, until the jelly thermometer reads 220° to 222°, or until the syrup sheets when dropped from a spoon (2 drops coming together and falling as 1 drop). This takes about 1-1/2 hours. Ladle into hot, sterilized jars and seal immediately according to directions in Chapter 1.
Makes approximately 6 half-pints.

The Bells of St. Clement's

ORANGES and Lemons Day is one of London's quainter observances. It is celebrated in the small church of St. Clement's Dane, snug between the Inns of Court and the Thames on the Strand. The ceremony is held each year near the end of March, and it is a children's service. The interior of the church is decorated with citrus fruit, strung from pew to pew. St. Clement's is one of London's oldest churches, built by grateful Danes under King Alfred the Great. Alfred had issued a dispensation whereby Danes who had married English girls were permitted to remain in Anglia and become British citizens. The church burned down in 1666, the year of The Great Fire, and was reconstructed in the same century by Sir Christopher Wren, London's greatest architect. It was his masterwork. St. Clement's was a casualty of the Nazi aerial blitz of 1940, but has since been restored.

Oranges and Lemons Day is rooted in the recent past. First celebrated in 1920, it is a modern revival of an ancient parish custom. Attendants at St. Clement's Inn, that part of the Inns of Court opposite the church, once a year called upon residents of the inn. They presented them with oranges and lemons, and were given gratuities in return. The custom inspired a folk tune known to every English child, and used by British Intelligence in its long-wave, coded broadcasts to the Continent in World War II. At the height of the Oranges and Lemons celebration today, the carillon rings out the familiar strain:

> Oranges and lemons, says the bells of St. Clemen's;
> You owe me five farthin's, says the bells of St. Martin's:
> When will you pay me, says the bells of Old Bailey,
> When will that be, says the bells of Stepney,
> I do not know, says the great bell of Bow.
> When I get rich, says the bells of Shoreditch,
> Here comes a candle to light you to bed,
> And here comes a chopper to chop off your head.

VIII Preserves

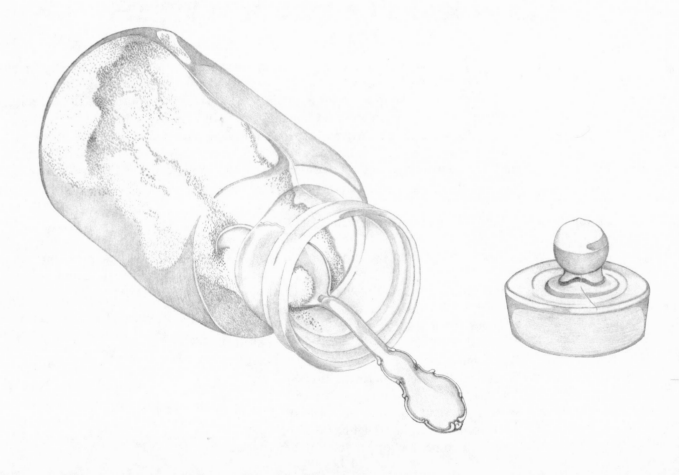

The Magnificent Grafter

S UCH WAS THE FAME of Luther Burbank, that when mendacious railroad conductors identified Burbank, California as his place of residence, the travelers were impressed. Actually, this appendage to Los Angeles was named after a New Hampshire-born dentist. Yet even the usually accurate *New York Times* had the famed Scottish balladeer and comic, Sir Harry Lauder, visiting the great man in Burbank, California. Sir Harry did indeed visit him, as did Henry Ford, Thomas Edison, Paderewski, Madame Schumann-Heink, Harvey Firestone, Helen Keller, John Burroughs, William Jennings Bryan, Jack London, John Muir and Red Grange. But the visit was paid 400 miles to the north of Burbank, in the then small town of Santa Rosa, about 20 miles above San Francisco.

Burbank was a native of Massachusetts, and had scored his first success before coming West by developing the Burbank potato. He was 26 when he rode the day coach across the continent, his rail trip terminating in San Francisco. He was awed by the city and the clement weather, but appalled by the drinking habits of its people. One day while searching for a glass of water, then hard to come by in that sinful city, he vowed he would never drink spirits, a vow he kept.

Burbank had chosen Santa Rosa because he had been told it had the most equable climate in the United States. The fact that a brother already lived there may have influenced his decision. Burbank acquired four acres of ground and soon was at work breeding plants. Warren Dutton, a Santa Rosa banker, wanted to plant a prune orchard because the dried fruit could be shipped East at a handsome profit. He wanted a 20,000-tree orchard in eight months, although the prune seed took 18 months to set. Burbank turned his deft hand to the project. He took the fast-growing almond seed of the same family and grafted prune buds onto the growing almond trees. He then broke the tops of the almond twigs and left them hanging so they were still a host, but most of the strength of the tree flowed to the prune bud. At the end of the eight-month period he delivered to Dutton 19,500 prune saplings, and the banker did not press for the other 500. The accomplishment made Burbank's name known to farmers throughout California. In 1893, the publication of his book, *New Creations in Fruits and Flowers,* established his name and reputation throughout the world.

Some of Burbank's creations were more exercises in versatility than commercial ventures. When a friend bet he could not make a white blackberry, Burbank proceeded to do so. It ripened to the color of ice. In like manner he developed the plumcot, a cross between the plum and the apricot, and mated a strawberry to a raspberry. But these were diversions; his lasting accomplishments included the Elberta peach, the Flaming Gold nectarine, the Beauty, the El Dorado and the Santa Rosa plum, to name a few.

111

The Santa Rosa plum spread to Europe, Africa and Australia, and today accounts for one-third of the plum varieties planted.

Had Burbank been able to patent his new hybrids, he would have become many times a millionaire, but the present plant patent law was not enacted until 1930, four years after his death. In his lifetime he was to lament, "A man can patent a mousetrap or copyright a nasty song, but if he gives to the world a new fruit that will add millions to the value of the earth's annual harvests, he will be fortunate if he is rewarded by so much as having his name connected with the result."

One of the great man's more bizarre developments was the spineless cactus, on which he lavished time and attention until the plant was as smooth as polished soapstone. Burbank foresaw cattle grazing through all of the arid places of the world, sustained by the spineless cactus. He built a 14-room house in Santa Rosa through the sale of five leaves of his cactus for propagation to an Australian rancher. Though widely promoted, the spineless cactus, his greatest dream, was his greatest failure. In 1908, the United States Department of Agriculture pronounced the cactus was unable to do more than sustain itself with rainfall or artificial watering, and declared that Burbank's cactus could not withstand the hardships of desert life.

Burbank had his detractors in scientific circles, largely because he kept no detailed records of his experiments, preferring to spend his days grafting and budding until he stumbled onto success. One wag went so far as to suggest that Luther Burbank had crossed the eggplant with the milkweed to create an omelet plant. And in the Preparedness Days before the United States' entry into World War I, Burbank followed the pacifist line, which prompted General Leonard Wood to remark, "Oh, yes. Isn't he the man who developed the spineless cactus?"

The Burbank *modus operandi* was to have hundreds of experiments underway at a given time. By grafting near the top of the branches rather than near the trunk, he had as many as 500 varieties of fruit growing on a tree at one time. Most of his attempts at hybridizing failed, yet over his working lifetime more than 800 of his new plants were introduced, or an average of one every three weeks. A friend with a mathematical turn of mind, surveying a pile of grafting twigs, estimated that Burbank could sell his grafting wood for $800,000 a cord.

Luther Burbank's first marriage was to a Denver girl who had taken his fancy on a trip to the East. It lasted eight years, most of them miserable. She preferred an active social life, which Luther's working habits precluded. She became a nag, a virago, and later was prone to pelting him with crockery. One night, when she prowled the house seeking a gun to shoot him, Burbank moved out to the stable. He divorced her in 1896. Several years later, he received a letter from a man who had subsequently married her, with the plaintive note, "How did you get rid of her?" Burbank's second marriage, to his secretary, was a happier union; he was 67, she in her mid-twenties, sweet of disposition and devoted to the man and his work.

Although fame embraced Burbank, fortune eluded him. Basically, the great plant breeder served as a wholesaler to nurserymen, and his profits were not great. Two ventures into which he was cajoled by promoters were financial disasters. A book publisher contracted to publish his writings in a series of

112

volumes. Since the writings consisted of a series of notes tucked in drawers throughout the house, Burbank spent the next seven to eight years compiling and editing them, working late into the night on top of his heavy daily work schedule. Shortly after he had completed the manuscript, the publishing house went out of business owing him almost $100,000, by his account. Later, a seed company undertook to distribute the products of his farm. An elaborate office was opened, many people put on the payroll and a cadre of salesmen and officers were organized at portly salaries "for everyone but myself," rued Burbank. But the entrepreneurs had no knowledge of the business, and the company went into receivership, costing Burbank "a good many thousands of dollars."

Luther Burbank was a disciple of Darwin, and extended Darwin's theories to the human species. "If civilization is to endure, some way must be found to produce more of the fit and fewer of the unfit." Burbank had strong views on other subjects. "The crowding of our cities is like the crowding of a neglected garden, and that is where spindling, weak, attenuated growth appears. . . . The growth of cities is unhealthy for a nation, but I see a tendency to spread out into suburbs and outlying districts that may solve a problem that has caused disaster in past history."

Near the end of his life, Burbank aroused great controversy when he was quoted in an Oakland paper as professing to be an infidel, that Christ himself was an infidel. The telegraph wires spread the statement across the nation and cables carried it around the world. The public outcry was great and he received many venomous letters. His friends begged him to relent. He retracted, but only partially; he acknowledged there was some force that controlled the world but he refused to personalize it. A few years later, in 1926, the great hybridizer suffered a heart attack, and 20 days later he was dead. The city of Santa Rosa granted special permission that he be buried under the cedar of Lebanon in the yard of the old cottage where he had first lived. It was a tree Burbank had grown from seed shortly after arriving in California.

Preserves

BAR-LE-DUC

This is better than syrup
for pancakes and waffles.

5 pounds of black currants
10 cups of sugar (5 pounds)

Wash and pick over currants; then cook them slowly in a preserving kettle until the juice is extracted, about 15 minutes. Add the sugar, bring slowly to a boil and boil rapidly until thick, about 20 minutes. Skim with a metal spoon. Ladle into hot, sterilized jars and seal immediately according to directions in Chapter 1.
Makes approximately 10 half-pints.

APRICOT PRESERVES

*Appetizing served as a dessert
with sour cream
when apricot season is long past.*

2 pounds of underripe apricots
4 cups of sugar (2 pounds)
Juice of 2 lemons

Wash, blanch, peel, halve and pit the apricots. Mix apricots thoroughly with the sugar and lemon juice and cover tightly. Let stand 4 to 5 hours in the refrigerator. Place the fruit mixture in a preserving kettle and bring slowly to a boil until the sugar dissolves, stirring occasionally. Cook rapidly until the fruit is clear and transparent, about 30 minutes. As mixture thickens, stir frequently to prevent sticking. Ladle into hot, sterilized jars and seal immediately as directed in Chapter 1.
Makes approximately 4 half-pints.

SPICED PRESERVED CANTALOUPE

Delicious quick dessert with sour cream.

2 large ripe cantaloupes
2 cups of sugar (1 pound)
1 cup of water
1/2 cup of cider vinegar
1 6-inch stick of cinnamon
4 whole cloves

Peel and seed the cantaloupes and cut into 1-inch squares. Place it in a preserving kettle with the sugar, water, vinegar and spices. Slowly bring the mixture to a boil over medium heat, then lower the heat and simmer until the melon is tender. Remove the melon with a slotted spoon and simmer the syrup for 5 minutes longer. Fill the lower half of 2 hot, sterilized pint jars with the melon and fill with the syrup. Seal immediately according to directions in Chapter 1.
Makes 2 pints.

Preserves

PRESERVED MORELLO CHERRIES

5 pounds of Morello cherries
4-1/2 pounds of cubed sugar

Wash cherries and remove seeds, losing as little juice as possible. Put the cherries into a preserving kettle, cover them with half of the sugar and let stand for 2 hours. Add the remaining sugar and boil gently, skimming frequently, until the fruit is clear and the syrup thick, about 20 to 30 minutes. Ladle into hot, sterilized jars and seal immediately according to directions in Chapter 1.
Makes approximately 8 pints.

DRUNKARD'S CHERRIES

Serve these as you would
bonbons or mints with demitasse.

3-1/2 pounds of large black cherries
6-3/4 cups of sugar (3-3/8 pounds)
Brandy

Wash and pit cherries and put them into a preserving kettle. Cover with sugar and let stand for 2 hours. Then cook them slowly over low heat, uncovered, for about 25 minutes or until the cherries are tender. Remove the fruit with a slotted spoon and set aside; cook the syrup until it is thickened, about 20 minutes. Measure the syrup and add 5 tablespoons of brandy to the kettle for each cup of syrup. Return the fruit to the kettle. Ladle into hot, sterilized jars and seal immediately according to directions in Chapter 1.
Makes approximately 12 half-pints.

PRESERVED DAMASCUS FIGS

4 pounds of ripe black figs
1-1/2 teaspoons of whole cloves
1 cinnamon stick
1 cup of cider vinegar
3 tablespoons of freshly squeezed lemon juice
3-1/2 cups of sugar (1-3/4 pounds)

Wash and stem the figs. Place figs in a saucepan and add water to just cover fruit. Bring this to a boil, then lower heat and simmer uncovered for 20 minutes. Drain the water and set fruit aside. Tie cloves and cinnamon stick in a cheesecloth bag. In a preserving kettle, put the cheesecloth bag, vinegar, lemon juice and sugar. Boil the syrup for about 30 minutes until it registers 220° to 222° on your jelly thermometer, or until it sheets when dropped from a spoon (2 drops coming together and falling from the spoon as 1 drop). When the syrup is ready, add the figs and cook them gently for about 10 more minutes. Remove the cheesecloth bag and discard. Ladle into hot, sterilized jars and seal immediately according to directions in Chapter 1. Makes approximately 6 pints.

WHITE FIG PRESERVES

Rolled in prosciutto with a toothpick,
these make a marvelous antipasto hors d'oeuvre.

3-1/2 pounds of ripe white figs
1-1/2 teaspoons of whole cloves
1 cinnamon stick
3/4 cup of cider vinegar
1 tablespoon of freshly squeezed orange juice
3 cups of sugar (1-1/2 pounds)

Wash and stem the figs. Barely cover them with water and simmer uncovered for 20 minutes until tender. Drain well and set figs aside. Tie the spices into a cheesecloth bag and combine with vinegar, orange juice and sugar in a preserving kettle. Boil gently, uncovered, until syrup registers 220° to 222° on your jelly thermometer, or until the syrup sheets when dropped from a spoon (2 drops come together and fall as 1 drop). Add figs and cook for 10 minutes. Remove and discard the spice bag. Ladle the figs and syrup into hot, sterilized jars and seal immediately according to directions in Chapter 1.
Makes approximately 5 pints.

Preserves

KIWI PRESERVES

Delicious topping for many exotic desserts.

2-1/2 pounds of kiwi berries
Juice of 1 lemon
4 cups of sugar (2 pounds)
1 cup of water

Wash and peel kiwi berries and cut them into quarters. Sprinkle the lemon juice over the fruit and let stand 1 hour. In a preserving kettle, combine fruit, sugar and water. Bring slowly to a boil until sugar dissolves, about 15 minutes. Cook fruit until tender; remove fruit with a slotted spoon and set aside. Cook syrup rapidly until thick, about 15 minutes, stirring frequently. Place fruit in hot, sterilized jars. Ladle syrup into jars to cover fruit and seal immediately as directed in Chapter 1.
Makes approximately 5 half-pints.

KUMQUAT PRESERVES

2 pounds of kumquats
1-1/2 tablespoons of baking soda
4 cups of sugar (2 pounds)
Boiling water

Wash kumquats and sprinkle with baking soda. Cover with 4 cups of boiling water and let stand until water is cool. Then pour off water and rinse fruit thoroughly 2 or 3 times under cold water. Drain well and prick each kumquat to prevent them from bursting. Have enough boiling water to cover fruit in preserving kettle and drop in kumquats. Cook about 15 minutes, or until tender. Remove kumquats with a slotted spoon, draining well, and set aside. Add sugar to the water in the kettle and boil together for about 10 minutes. Add drained kumquats and cook until fruit is clear and transparent. Remove from heat and, using a slotted spoon, carefully place fruit on flat trays. Pour syrup over fruit and let stand overnight; this will plump the kumquats. The next morning, reheat kumquats in their syrup. Ladle into hot, sterilized jars and seal immediately according to directions in Chapter 1.
Makes approximately 4 pints.

PRESERVED MANGOES

*Chilled and served in fruit cocktail glasses
with a dollop of whipped cream,
these make a quick and intriguing dessert.*

2-1/2 pounds of ripe mangoes
4 cups of sugar (2 pounds)
1 cup of water

Wash and peel the mangoes; cut pulp from the seeds in thick lengthwise strips and set aside. Boil the sugar and water in a preserving kettle over medium heat until it measures 220° to 222° on the jelly thermometer, or until syrup sheets when dropped from a spoon (2 drops coming together and falling as 1 drop). Gently place the mango slices in the syrup, trying not to break them, and boil over medium heat until transparent, about 10 minutes. Ladle into hot, sterilized jars and seal immediately according to directions in Chapter 1. Makes approximately 4 pints.

PEACH PRESERVES

A wonderful winter dessert treat with cookies.

4-1/2 pounds of underripe peaches
3/4 cup of water
6 cups of sugar (3 pounds)

Wash, blanch and peel the peaches. Slice fruit away from the pit, obtaining all of the fruit possible. In a preserving kettle, cook the peaches in the water for about 5 minutes, or until barely tender. Keep the heat low to prevent scorching. Remove the peaches from the kettle with a slotted spoon and set aside. Add the sugar to the juice. Boil the juice for about 20 minutes, until the syrup sheets when dropped from a spoon (2 drops coming together and falling as 1 drop), or until it measures 220° to 222° on a jelly thermometer. Add the peaches to the syrup and cook very rapidly for 12 minutes. Remove from heat and skim with a metal spoon. Ladle into hot, sterilized jars and seal immediately according to directions in Chapter 1. Makes approximately 7 pints.

Preserves

PEAR PRESERVES

A great dessert following ham or pork.

2 pounds of medium-ripe pears (about 6 medium-
    size pears)
1 lemon
3 cups of sugar (1-1/2 pounds)
3 cups of water

Wash, pare, core and quarter the pears and set aside. Wash and slice the lemon wafer thin, eliminating the seeds; set aside. Combine 1-1/2 cups of the sugar and 3 cups of water in a preserving kettle and boil for 2 minutes. Add the pears and boil gently for 15 minutes. Add remaining 1-1/2 cups of sugar and the reserved lemon slices, stirring until the sugar has dissolved. Cook rapidly until the fruit is clear, about 25 minutes. Remove from heat, cover and let stand 24 hours in a cool place. Pick out the fruit and divide it into 5 hot, sterilized half-pint jars. Cook the syrup for 5 to 10 minutes. Then pour syrup boiling hot over the fruit and seal immediately according to directions in Chapter 1. Makes approximately 5 half-pints.

PRESERVED STRAWBERRIES

*This makes a wonderful
winter strawberry shortcake.*

2 pounds of strawberries
4 cups of sugar (2 pounds)
1/3 cup of freshly squeezed lemon juice

Wash and hull the strawberries. Place alternate layers of berries and sugar in a preserving kettle and let stand 3 to 4 hours. Now heat very slowly until the sugar has dissolved, stirring as little as possible to keep the berries whole. Over high heat, boil the preserves rapidly for 15 to 20 minutes, stirring gently to prevent burning. Now add lemon juice and cook 2 more minutes. Ladle into hot, sterilized jars and seal immediately according to directions in Chapter 1.
Makes approximately 3 pints.

SPICED TOMATO PRESERVES

A very special treat with cold meat.

3 pounds of green tomatoes
1 pound of red tomatoes
2 lemons
5 cups of sugar (2-1/2 pounds)
1/2 teaspoon of whole cloves
Half of a 3-inch stick of cinnamon

Wash and blanch the tomatoes; peel and cut them into quarters. Wash and thinly slice the lemons, discarding the seeds. Place the tomatoes and lemons in a preserving kettle and add the sugar and spices. Bring to a boil and then lower the heat. Simmer slowly uncovered until thick, about 1-1/2 hours, stirring occasionally to prevent scorching. Ladle into hot, sterilized jars and seal immediately according to directions in Chapter 1.
Makes approximately 8 half-pints.

Preserves

GREEN TOMATO PRESERVES

6 pounds of green tomatoes
Boiling water
8 cups of sugar (4 pounds)
3 lemons

Wash and slice the tomatoes and place them in a preserving kettle; cover with boiling water and boil for 5 minutes. Drain off liquid. Add the sugar to the tomatoes; cover and let stand for 3 hours. Remove tomatoes with a slotted spoon and set aside. Boil the syrup over high heat until it sheets when dropped from a spoon (2 drops coming together and falling as 1 drop), or until a jelly thermometer reads 220° to 222°. Wash and slice the lemons wafer thin; discard the seeds. Add lemon slices and reserved tomatoes to the syrup. Boil rapidly for about 10 minutes until the fruit is clear. Ladle into hot, sterilized jars and seal immediately according to directions in Chapter 1.
Makes approximately 6 pints.

TOMATO-GINGER PRESERVES

2 pounds of small tomatoes
3 cups of sugar (1-1/2 pounds)
3 lemons
4 teaspoons of chopped preserved ginger

Wash, blanch and peel the tomatoes. Cover them with the sugar and let stand overnight in a covered bowl. In the morning, drain off the juice and set the tomatoes aside. Boil the juice over medium heat in an uncovered preserving kettle until the syrup sheets from a spoon (2 drops coming together and falling as 1 drop), or until a jelly thermometer reads 220° to 222°. Wash and slice the lemons very thinly, discarding the seeds. Add the lemon slices, tomatoes and chopped ginger to the syrup. Cook uncovered over medium heat until the juice is thick and the tomatoes are transparent, about 40 minutes. Ladle into hot, sterilized jars and seal immediately according to directions in Chapter 1.
Makes about 6 half-pints.

Feeding the Four Hundred

A VISITOR to the gorges of Wall Street is often led by his host to lunch at Delmonico's. The name strikes a cord, and he imagines he is dining at *the* Delmonico's, especially if he is an *auslander*. Not true, since the original Delmonico's closed its door in 1923. The present Delmonico's at Beaver and South William Streets is authentic in one respect; it occupies the site of one of the original Delmonico's. The decor is *fin de siècle,* the food good, and reservations are recommended.

The Beaver and South William Street address was the second of the numerous restaurants the Delmonicos opened. The year was 1837, and the restaurant was modest in size and appointments. The Delmonico family moved, as New York moved, steadily uptown to pursue their patronage. They opened a second restaurant at Broadway and Chambers Street, opposite City Hall, retaining the Beaver and South William establishment to serve the lunch-time appetites of the Wall Street trade.

Again New York, later to be the borough of Manhattan, shifted uptown, and the Delmonico's with it, to Fifth Avenue and Fourteenth Street. There were now three Delmonico's restaurants operating full bore. The next move was to the junction of Broadway and Fifth at Madison Square. The last move was to Fifth Avenue and Forty-fourth Street, where the famous name attracted the *haut ton* until the doors closed in 1923. Prohibition, the jazz age and its speakeasies, the high price of serving a good meal are all blamed for the demise of this world-famous institution.

The Delmonicos were Swiss-Italian, emigrating to America from the southernmost of Switzerland's cantons. Their first venture in New York was a cafe and pastry shop in 1827, which means the continuity of the family business reached 96 years, a remarkable record for the capricious restaurant business.

One of the more memorable evenings in the many at Delmonico's occurred in 1868, when Charles Dickens came to America for his second reading tour. After his first tour in 1842, he had returned to England and wrote in his *American Notes* of the savage eating habits of Americans and the barbarous cuisine. His second tour ended with a $15-a-plate dinner at Delmonico's with Horace Greeley as toastmaster. Dickens withdrew his remarks of 25 years earlier and said, "Wherever I have been, in the smallest places equally with the largest, I have been received with unsurpassable politeness, delicacy, sweet temper, hospitality, consideration. . . ."

Lorenzo Delmonico, who with the suave Charles was the most dominant of the clan, almost lost the business in the 1850's when he strayed into the Wall Street bypaths. Discovery of oil in Pennsylvania led to widespread speculation in oil stocks. Lorenzo invested in and became president of a company drilling for oil in Brooklyn! Upon returning from a visit to Switzerland, he found that, thanks to his oil venture, he was ruined. He was forced to put the Delmonico's restaurants up for sale. Wall Street was not about to see its favorite restaurants shuttered; on the day of the auction, no bids were submitted. So Delmonico's, and Lorenzo, survived, the latter helped by advances from friends.

The fame of Delmonico's during its middle and later years was due more to one man than any others. His name was Ward McAllister. This vain, pompous little man was appalled by the inroads made on New York society by the ill-mannered newly rich. He began his campaign with a series of cotillon balls at Delmonico's. Later he formed a group known as the Patriarch's, to pass upon the social pretensions of those trying to crash the charmed circle. A Patriarch, to qualify, must be a fourth-generation American; McAllister even singled out the Patriarchs, who were 25 in number. These worthies passed upon who might attend the three annual balls which separated the "in" from the "out." At a ball for Mrs. Astor, the guest list finally approved by McAllister came to 400, and thence the name "The 400" for the socially elect.

When Charles Delmonico succeeded Lorenzo, who died in a hunting accident, one of his steady patrons was a sea captain named Ben Wenberg. He brought back from one voyage a new way to cook lobster, and demonstrated it to Charles. The restaurateur was delighted, and *lobster à la Wenburg* appeared on his menu. Later Wenburg and Delmonico had a falling out, and by transposition the dish, famous ever since, has been *lobster à la Newberg*.

With Delmonico's at its height, a rival, Rector's, appeared upon the scene. Like Delmonico's, it staked its reputation on the finest French cuisine. It was especially popular with the theatrical crowd, and an after-theater table downstairs was a mark of status. Rector's became so famous it needed no sign on its facade; everyone who was anyone knew where it was. The interior was floor-to-ceiling glass, crystal chandeliers and green and gold decor. At its height, the headwaiters were reported to have received $20,000 in Christmas tips.

George Rector, son of the founder, was *maître d'* and social arbiter at Rector's. Florenz Ziegfeld dined there frequently with his French import and wife, Anna Held. In her first Broadway musical, Anna became the toast of New York for the suggestive song, *Won't You Come and Play Wiz Me.* Ziegfeld encouraged the rumor spreading around that his Anna bathed daily in fresh cow's milk. The memory of Anna Held that lingers longest is her supposed milk baths.

The most famous theatrical group to be squired into Rector's was the Floradora Sextette. These lovelies had the easiest act in town; yet were the rage. On stage with six young men, they managed a few routine steps, at which point the men asked, "Tell me, pretty maiden, are there any more at home like you?" To which the Sextette answered coyly, "There are a few, kind sir." A few more steps and the act was over, and the audience ecstatic. All six of the original Sextette married millionaires, among them a nephew of Andrew Carnegie. At least, so it is said. One of them is believed to have made it on her own through a stock tip by a Morgan partner.

One of the most memorable battles at Rector's was the contest between Möet & Chandon and Mumm's champagnes. The salesman for Möet & Chandon would send two complimentary bottles of his product to distinguished diners, to be topped by three complimentary bottles sent over by his competitor. Or Mumm's might get the first drop to be topped by Möet & Chandon. Since both salesmen prospered, the complimentary bottles must have merely wetted the whistles of diners at Rector's.

Flo Ziegfeld's first in a long line of follies was the "Follies of 1907." Among the tunes in the libretto was *If the Tables at Rector's Could Talk*. The tune is long forgotten, and Rector's a dim memory, yet if the tables at Rector's could talk, what great stories they could tell.

IX Honey Preserves

The Busy Bees

U NTIL THE ARRIVAL of the sugarcane from China via India and the Middle East, honey had been the principal sweetener of the Western world from prehistoric times. Volumes can be and have been written about it. Pythagoras lived exclusively on bread and honey and died at age 90; his disciple, Apollonius, reached 130 years. The apiary was treasured not only for its honey, but also for its wax; it was the chief source of candles to illuminate the dark nights of earlier times. Tickner Edwardes, author and beekeeper, wrote, "Among the Anglo-Saxons the beehives supplied the whole nation, from the King down to the poorest serf, not only with an important part of their food but with drink and light as well." The drink was the honey-brew, mead.

Dr. Bodog B. Beck, in his book *Honey and Health,* credits honey with the reprieve from the grave and the subsequent longevity of Luigi Cornaro. Luigi was the scion of an illustrious family. The Cornari were among the first 12 patrician families of the Venetian Republic, which for centuries provided military tribunes for the state. Many of the family were members of the first Great Council of Venice, established in 1172. The Cornaro family contributed a queen and four princely doges to the Republic, as well as 22 procurators to St. Marks and nine cardinals to the church. In the magnificent Gothic church of Santi Giovanni e Paolo, the Westminster Abbey of Venice, lies the imposing mausoleum of Doge Marco Cornaro.

Luigi was a prodigal of the family. His dissipations and intemperance deprived him of honors and privileges his family traditionally held. By age 35, his health was broken and his physicians despaired of him. One of them prescribed the lightest diet as his only recourse. Cornaro seized at the advice, and his health turned. He lived on 12 ounces of solid food and 13 ounces of liquid a day; his diet consisted of bread, light broth, eggs, veal, fowl, birds and fish. (Not at a single sitting, of course.) His only sweet was honey. On this lean diet he regained his health, his *élan,* and the honors and privileges to which a Cornari was entitled. He became known as "The Temperate One"; he married and sired a daughter. At age 70, he was seriously injured when his carriage overturned. Doctors urged blood letting and strong medicine, but Luigi refused, and soon recovered without disability. At 80, friends prevailed upon him to escalate his diet to 14 ounces of food and 16 ounces of liquid. He did, became ill, and reverted to his old diet.

Luigi Cornaro is remembered for his autobiography *The Temperate Life,* published in four separate parts in his 83rd, 86th, 91st and 95th years. It hardly ranks with *The Confessions of St. Augustine,* and sensation seekers are advised to pass it up for more racy material, as it draws a veil over his intemperate life. In it he hails, "Divine Sobriety, pleasing to God, the friend of Nature, the daughter of reason, the sister of virtue, the companion of temperate living. . . ." At another point he proclaims, "I never knew the world was so beautiful until I reached old age." The book contains a few homilies which might be useful in the difficult years ahead. "Eat nothing but what is necessary to sustain life . . . A man cannot be a perfect physician to anyone, except to himself . . . As you grow older, eat less."

In his eighties and nineties, Cornaro still hiked, hunted, sang and wrote. He died peacefully at the age of 103. Cornaro is better known through Tintoretto's portrait of him in the Pitti Palace, Florence, or his striking *palazzo* in Padua, than for *The Temperate Life.*

Another instance of longevity, which may be attributed to honey, is the 90 years enjoyed by Marcus Terentius Varro. This soldier, politician and author was a beekeeper, and his account of the art of the apiarist in *Res Rustica* is the oldest we have. That he lived to 90 was itself miraculous; he campaigned with Pompey against Caesar, twice being pardoned by Caesar for backing the wrong general. Following Caesar's assassination, he fell under Marc Antony's proscription and his property and library were plundered. Varro was spared by the intervention of a friend and opted for the quiet life. Varro is credited with writing 620 books, of which nine survive. Visions of Dr. Eliot's "five-foot shelf" vanish when we learn the average book was 50 to 60 typeset pages.

Varro liked to write in the form of dialogue or conversations between people. So the pages in *Res Rustica* about bees consist of a chat between himself, Appius, Axius and Merula. We learn that bees are not of a solitary nature, like the eagle, but are like human beings. The bee has three tasks, food, dwelling and toil; and the food is not the same as the wax, nor the honey, nor the dwelling (hive). The chamber in the honeycomb has six angles, the same number as the bee has feet, and geometricians have proved that this hexagon inscribed in a circular figure encloses the greatest amount of space. Bees forage abroad, and within the hive they produce a substance which, because it is the sweetest of all, is acceptable to gods and men alike. Their commonwealth is like the states of men, for there is king, government and fellowship. Now here Varro and his colleagues err; what they call the king bee undoubtedly was the queen bee. But there is an old axiom, or there should be: Never quarrel with a beekeeper.

Beekeeping was profitable in ancient Rome and its colonies, Varro assures us. With Merula as the speaker, he writes, "As to the gain I have this to say . . . and I have as my authorities not only Seius, who has his apiaries let out for an annual rental of 5,000 sestertii, but also our friend Varro here. We have heard the latter tell the story that he had two soldiers under him in Spain . . . . They were well-off, because, though their father had left only a small villa and a bit of land certainly not larger than one *iugerum* [two-thirds acre], they had built an apiary entirely around the villa, and keep a garden. . . . These men never received less than 10,000 sestertii for their honey." This amounts to $400 in very round figures since it is impossible to translate an ancient currency into a modern; it is hard enough to exchange a modern for a modern.

In building an apiary, Varro advises, place it near the villa, in an area protected from echoes which might put the bees to flight. The air should be temperate, not too hot in summer, not without sun in winter. The owner should sow crops attractive to the bee. At the middle of the hive, small openings are made at the right and left, so the bees may enter and exit, and a small covered hole at the back, so the keeper can remove the cone. There should be clear water nearby for them to drink, preferably a shallow rillet. Since bees cannot go out in every kind of weather, food should be provided them so they will not have to live on honey alone. Boiled ripe figs placed near the hives are recommended.

"The time comes when bees are ready to swarm, which generally occurs when the well hatched new brood is over large and they wish to send out their young as it were a colony (just as the Sabines used to do on account of the number of their children)." The wise keeper at this juncture prepares a new hive, smears it with bee-bread and other balms that attract the bees, and blows smoke around them to encourage them to enter after they alight. It is a source of amazement that the art of the apiarist, trading a king for a queen, has changed so little over the centuries.

Honey Preserves

HONEY JELLY

2-1/2 cups of clover honey
3/4 cup of water
1/2 bottle of liquid pectin (3 ounces)
Juice of 1 lemon

In a large saucepan, combine honey and water and bring to a boil quickly. Add the pectin and bring to a full rolling boil. Stir in lemon juice and remove from the stove. Pour into hot, sterilized jars and seal immediately according to directions in Chapter 1.
Makes approximately 6 half-pints.

FIG-HONEY JAM

4 pounds of figs
2 lemons
6 cups of mild honey

Wash, peel and chop the figs; wash and chop the lemons, including the peel. Combine the fruits and the honey in a preserving kettle. Cook slowly uncovered, stirring frequently, over low heat until thick, about 1-1/2 hours. When thick, ladle into hot, sterilized jars and seal immediately according to directions in Chapter 1.
Makes approximately 12 half-pints.

LEMON CURD WITH HONEY

4 large lemons
4 whole eggs plus 2 egg yolks
1/4 pound of butter
2 cups of clover honey

Wash the lemons, squeeze and strain the juice and grate the rinds. Blend the eggs and egg yolks in a blender or beat by hand, and set aside. In a double boiler, melt the butter and add the honey. Gradually add the beaten eggs, lemon juice and rind. Stir over low heat until thick and creamy, about 25 minutes. Ladle into hot, sterilized jars and seal immediately according to directions in Chapter 1. This will keep for about 2 months in the refrigerator once it is opened.
Makes approximately 3 half-pints.

HONEY-LEMON JELLY

*Excellent for gifts to friends
with throat complaints or colds.
A welcome filling for tarts
served after fish.*

2-1/2 cups of mild honey
3/4 cup of warm water
1/2 bottle of liquid pectin (3 ounces)
3 tablespoons of freshly squeezed lemon juice

Combine honey and warm water in a preserving kettle and bring to a full rolling boil. Stir in the liquid pectin and boil for 2 minutes. Remove the jelly from the heat and stir in the lemon juice. Ladle immediately into hot, sterilized jars and seal according to directions in Chapter 1.
Makes approximately 6 half-pints.

Honey Preserves

HONEY-PEACH JAM

3 pounds of ripe peaches
7 cups of mild honey
Juice of 1 lemon
1 6-ounce bottle of liquid pectin

Wash, blanch, peel and pit the peaches. Chop or coarsely grind them through a food chopper. They should measure 5 cups, well packed. Mix fruit, honey and lemon juice together in a preserving kettle. Bring to a full rolling boil. Boil hard for 1 minute, stirring constantly. Remove from heat and immediately stir in liquid pectin. Return to heat and again bring to a full rolling boil. Boil hard 1 minute, stirring constantly. Remove from heat and skim off foam with a metal spoon. Alternately stir and skim about 5 minutes to cool slightly and to prevent fruit from floating. Ladle into hot, sterilized jars and seal immediately according to directions in Chapter 1.
Makes approximately 10 half-pints.

PEACH AND HONEY CHUTNEY

*Delicious with meat or curry,
and when used as a filling for an omelet
that is topped with sour cream.*

1-1/2 pounds of ripe peaches
1-1/2 pounds of green apples
2 pounds of tomatoes
1 medium-size green bell pepper
1 large onion
1 teaspoon of salt
1/2 teaspoon of ground ginger
1/2 teaspoon of whole mustard seeds
1/2 cup of red wine vinegar
3/4 cup of mild honey

Wash, blanch, peel, seed and dice the peaches. Wash, peel, core and dice the apples. (There should be 3 tightly packed cups of each.) Wash and chop the tomatoes and green pepper. Peel and chop the onion. Place all of the ingredients *except* the honey into a preserving kettle and bring to a full rolling boil. Reduce heat and boil for 30 minutes, stirring occasionally. Then gradually add the honey while stirring constantly. Lower the heat and simmer uncovered until mixture thickens, about 30 minutes. Ladle into hot, sterilized jars and seal immediately according to directions in Chapter 1. Refrigerate after jars are opened.
Makes approximately 6 half-pints.

HONEY, PEAR AND CHERRY CONSERVE

3 pounds of ripe Bartlett pears
1/4 cup of maraschino cherries
1/3 cup of maraschino cherry juice
6 lemon slices
3 tablespoons of freshly squeezed lemon juice
3 tablespoons of seedless white raisins
4 cups of mild honey
1 6-ounce bottle of liquid pectin

Wash, peel, core and coarsely chop the pears; the chopped pears should measure about 5 cups. Chop the maraschino cherries. Put all ingredients except the pectin into a preserving kettle. Bring the mixture to a full rolling boil and boil hard for 5 minutes, stirring occasionally to prevent scorching. Remove from heat and add the pectin immediately. Skim with a metal spoon, stirring at the same time to prevent the fruit from floating. Ladle into hot, sterilized jars and seal immediately according to directions in Chapter 1.
Makes approximately 7 half-pints.

PLUM BUTTER WITH HONEY

8 pounds of plums
Boiling water
4 cups of mild honey

Wash the plums and place them in a preserving kettle. Barely cover them with boiling water and cook slowly for about 20 minutes, until they are soft. Strain to make 8 cups of plum purée. Return the purée to the preserving kettle and bring to a boil. Add the honey and cook over medium heat until the butter is of spreading consistency. It will cook in 45 to 60 minutes; the cooking time will depend on the juice content of your fruit. When the butter is thick, ladle it into hot, sterilized jars and seal immediately according to directions in Chapter 1.
Makes approximately 10 half-pints.

Honey Preserves

HONEY-PINEAPPLE JAM

1 large ripe pineapple
3 tablespoons of freshly squeezed lemon juice
3 cups of mild honey
1/2 bottle of liquid pectin (3 ounces)

Peel and core the pineapple; remove the brown "eyes." Put pineapple through a meat grinder or mash it thoroughly. In a preserving kettle, place the crushed pineapple, lemon juice and honey, mixing well. Bring to a boil and simmer uncovered for 20 minutes. Remove from heat and add the liquid pectin. Again, bring the mixture to a boil and boil for 1 minute; then remove from heat. Skim with a metal spoon. Ladle into hot, sterilized jars and seal immediately according to directions in Chapter 1.
Makes approximately 6 half-pints.

(If you live where pineapple is unattainable, a 1-pound 4-1/2-ounce can of crushed pineapple may be used with the juice of 1 more lemon.)

STRAWBERRY-HONEY JAM

Delicious on freshly buttered biscuits.

2-1/4 pounds of ripe strawberries
1/4 cup of powdered pectin
5 cups of mild honey

Wash, hull and crush the strawberries completely, retaining all of the juice. Measure 4-1/2 cups of strawberries into a preserving kettle. Add the pectin, mixing together well. Place the kettle over high heat and bring it to a boil, stirring constantly. Quickly stir in the honey and bring the jam to a full rolling boil. Boil hard for 2 minutes, stirring constantly. Remove from the heat and skim with a metal spoon. Stir and skim for 5 minutes to cool it slightly. Ladle into hot, sterilized jars and seal immediately according to directions in Chapter 1. Keep at room temperature for 24 hours until thoroughly set.
Makes approximately 10 half-pints.

SPICY WINE-HONEY JELLY

2 cups of sherry
2 cups of mild honey
1/8 teaspoon of ground cinnamon
1/8 teaspoon of ground cloves
1/2 bottle of liquid pectin (3 ounces)

Combine sherry, honey, cinnamon and cloves in a preserving kettle and bring to a full rolling boil. Stir in the liquid pectin and bring it to a boil again for 2 minutes, stirring constantly. Remove from the heat and skim with a metal spoon. Pour into hot, sterilized jars and seal immediately according to directions in Chapter 1. Let stand at room temperature for 24 hours until well set.
Makes approximately 5 half-pints.

WINTER MINT AND HONEY JELLY

2 tablespoons of dried mint leaves
3/4 cup of boiling water
2-1/2 cups of mild honey
Green food coloring
1/2 bottle of liquid pectin (3 ounces)

Place the mint leaves in a bowl and pour the boiling water over them; cover and let stand about 20 minutes. Strain and add enough water to liquid to make 3/4 cup. In a pan, mix mint liquid and honey and heat to boiling, adding a couple of drops of food coloring. Now add pectin and bring to a full rolling boil, stirring constantly. Boil hard for 1 minute. Remove from heat and skim off foam with a metal spoon. Pour into hot, sterilized jars and seal immediately according to directions in Chapter 1.
Makes approximately 3 half-pints.

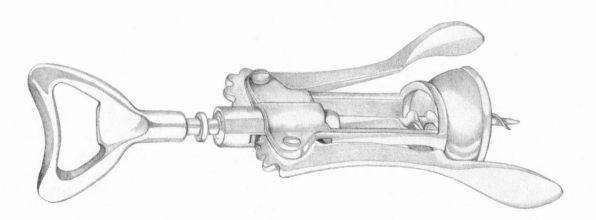

The Fruit of the Flightless Bird

THE KIWI has come to mean almost anything associated with New Zealand, from shoe polish to its soldiery to the fruit which bears the name. The kiwi is the official bird of the Dominion but, contrary to that hoary joke, not only does it not fly backwards, it does not fly at all. It is one of a number of flightless birds in New Zealand. (There is another species best described as semi-flightless, the kakapo parrot, which cannot lift off, but climbs a tree and glides to the ground.) The kiwi may be related to the now extinct moa, which grew as tall as 12 feet, exceeded in height only by the giraffe and elephant.

The flightless kiwi and moa lost their power of flight because there were no predators on New Zealand, neither man nor other carnivores. They had no reason to leave the ground. It was the arrival of Maoris in their long Polynesian canoes that led to extinction of the moa and the decimation of the kiwi. One moa provided a feast for an entire Maori tribe. The kiwi was hunted both for its flesh and its feathers, the latter prized for ceremonial cloaks. However, the belief the kiwi is nearing extinction is false. Two things preserved this remarkable bird: The kiwi is absolutely protected by the New Zealand government, and it is a bird of nocturnal habits, which explains why the Maoris, with their sunup to sundown life style, did not gorge him out of existence. Few residents of the isles ever get to see one in its natural state.

The kiwi stands about a foot tall, has a long bill, short legs and dumpy body, covered with soft-textured feathers. He inhabits the natural forests of North and South Islands and Stewart Islands, and sleeps by day in hollow logs or crevices, forages by night for worms, insects and berries. Since absolute protection was decreed, he has grown less reclusive, and is sometimes seen on the fringes of farmlands. The kiwi's feathers are treasured as trout flies, which explains why the stuffed kiwis on display in museums and in New Zealand consulates around the world are enclosed in tough, plastic cases, to discourage anglers from stripping them as bare as a plucked chicken.

The kiwi berry was named for its resemblance to the kiwi, furry and brown in appearance. In size it is somewhat larger than a very large grade AA egg. The berry is also known as the Chinese gooseberry, for it was introduced into New Zealand from the Yangtze Valley of China about 1906. The price of the berry is comparable to a T-bone steak, and has induced some adventurous growers in the United States to begin cultivation. In the United States, a single kiwi berry costs 25 cents and up at this writing, compared with 25 cents a pound in New Zealand, each pound having four or five berries, depending on size. Cultivation in the United States is limited, but in the past few years has grown from a few dozen acres to more than 2,000 acres, most of them in California. The enticement, of course, is the very high return on mature trees.

What keeps everyone from cashing in his Treasury bills or withdrawing his savings certificates and leaping into the kiwi-berry business headlong, is the high initial cost of planting. To raise an acre of kiwis to the production stage, generally the third year, requires $1,500 an acre, excluding land and the overhead sprinkler system required to simulate the light but frequent rains of New Zealand and to ward off frosts. An additional $500 must go into the trellis work to support the kiwi vines. The kiwi is susceptible to plant diseases, notably crown rot; the berry demands a lot of attention, and is a working, rather than a gentleman farmer's fruit.

The kiwi berry was first introduced into California about 1906, roughly the same time it was brought into New Zealand. But like its namesake bird in New Zealand, it never got off the ground. More than two decades ago a new variety of the kiwi berry was developed by the United States Department of Agriculture's Plant Introduction Station in Chico, California, a small, sun-baked town serving farmers in the Sacramento Valley. The U.S.D.A. station in Chico is now closed, but the kiwi is firmly rooted in California, thanks largely to Calchico Kiwi Company, mother hen to the developing industry; Calchico offers seedling-to-market assistance to its customers.

In the United States, the kiwi plant blooms in May after the last frosts are well behind, is harvested in November, and in recent years, has been sold out by February. In June, the New Zealand berries come into the American market as winter approaches in the Southern Hemisphere; they are snapped up in short order.

What is this curious delicacy that entices the homemaker to part with 25 cents or more per berry? Beneath the furry brown skin is a fruit that is pleasing to the eye and a delight to the palate. The kiwi shades from a dark green on the outside to beige at the center, and has a sweet and sour taste often described as a blend of strawberry, peach, gooseberry and rhubarb. The fruit is low in calories, high in vitamin C and in iron. If this sounds like some of the nostrums peddled on prime-time television, so be it. Its enzymes aid digestion and in New Zealand its juice is used extensively as a meat tenderizer.

The kiwi fruit shares one attribute with the kiwi bird. One male vine must be planted for every eight female vines, and the male plant produces no fruit. The male kiwi bird on his part performs such menial chores as nest building and hatching the enormous eggs in a two and one-half month period, during which he loses a third of his five-pound weight. He can draw some comfort that it is his shrill call, *kee-wee, kee-wee,* unmatched by the females, that gave this quaint bird its name.

X Desserts & Sauces

A Toast to Melba

I T IS REGRETTABLE that the great coloratura soprano, Mme. Nellie Melba, is better remembered today for Melba toast than for that divine dessert near the bottom of our poster-sized menus, peach Melba. Both were the creations of the masterful French chef, Auguste Escoffier. Rightfully, the toast should bear the name Ritz, since it was created by Escoffier for Marie Ritz, the wife of the celebrated innkeeper Cesar Ritz. Mme. Ritz had complained to Escoffier, then *chef de cuisine* at the Savoy Hotel in London, about the thickness of the toast commonly served; she would prefer something more delicate, less chewy. The resourceful Escoffier prepared a piece of toast, halved the slice by cutting through the crust, then reheated it. The wife of his great friend and business partner was delighted. Several years later, Mme. Melba returned from a long concert tour of America, and brought back to England, along with her steamer trunks, some excess weight. She went on a diet, a part of which was the thin, brittle toast created for Mme. Ritz. It was not long before Escoffier's creation bore the name Melba toast.

Mme. Melba was jealous of her name, even though it was not her own. She finally took out a patent on the name after seeing a Perfume Melba in a New York shop. The Australian songbird was born Nellie Mitchell in a suburb of Melbourne, the daughter of a prosperous brickmaker and contractor. She became Nellie Mitchell Armstrong after her marriage to Charles Armstrong, the handsome son of an Irish baronet. Marriage to Armstrong meant living in the bush, and life in the bush and its overpowering isolation soon began to pall. She left Armstrong shortly after the birth of her first and only son, George. In 1886, her father was appointed by the Australian government the Victorian Commissioner of the Indian and Colonial Exhibition to be held in London that year. He took his daughter with him.

Nellie had sung in Australia, and her concerts drew high praise from the colonial critics. Her father remained sceptical of a concert career. In England, he relented and gave her his blessings for a trip to Paris to visit the renowned teacher of voice, Mme. Mathilde Marchesi, with the understanding that if Mme. Marchesi did not give her high grades, the singing career was to be forgotten. After the audition with Mme. Marchesi, in which the wide-ranging voice reached a high F—two and a half tones above a high C—the teacher ran from the room and announced to her husband, "We have found a star."

But the teacher was unhappy with the name: Nellie Armstrong simply did not wash, nor did Nellie Mitchell. Marchesi probed into the singer's antecedents, her origins. Nellie mentioned she came from Melbourne. She suggested several plays upon the name, until—eureka—she hit upon the name Melba. Mme. Melba began her career in Brussels, a waypoint on the opera circuit akin to New Haven in the American theater. She was an immediate success, but later opened at the Covent Garden in London to mixed reviews.

So it was back to Brussels, more successes, then to a series of triumphs at the Paris Opera, and finally a return to Covent Garden to general critical applause.

One critic who had reservations about her talent was Corno di Bassetto of the *London Star,* the pseudonym of an opinionated young journalist, George Bernard Shaw. Mme. Melba was even less endowed with acting ability than most opera singers. A friend observed if she wished to show a strong emotion, she thrust up one arm; if she wanted to express very deep emotions, she threw up both arms. A new York critic went further: He wrote that Nellie had the voice of a nightingale, and to judge by her acting, the soul of one as well. Yet Nellie worked hard at the dramatic aspect of opera, and if she did not reach the height of art of the greatest divas, her voice more than compensated for it.

Nellie made millions during her career, commanding the highest fees during one of the happier times in world history. There were command performances before crowned heads, there was the company and the friendship of the most illustrious in the arts, the nobility, and even the giants of commerce. John Mackay, the silver baron and later co-founder of the Commercial Cable Company, granted her free cable privileges anywhere in the world. Nellie lived grandly, although not extravagantly, and her return and tour of Australia in 1902 was a major event in that country's short history.

The friendship between the chef Escoffier and Melba was of long standing, beginning at the Savoy in London, continuing at the Carlton in London, an even more elegant caravansary raised by Cesar Ritz, and finally to the Ritz Hotel on the Place Vendôme in Paris, the apogee of Cesar Ritz's dreams. It was at the Savoy where Escoffier created a dessert which keeps the name Melba fresh in the minds of epicures the world over. There are two versions of how it came about: one, Melba's, in her autobiography *Melodies and Memories* and the other Escoffier's, in his memoirs. According to Melba, the chef one day sent her a delicious peach nestled in a bed of ice cream. She asked the name of the dessert and was told peach Melba. The Escoffier version is more romantic and more widely accepted. Escoffier was a frequent theater and opera patron. One day the diva gave him two tickets to the opera, in which she performed in *Lohengrin.* One of the more striking scenes in *Lohengrin* is when the Prince is led on stage by a great swan. The day after the performance, Melba invited friends for dinner. When it came time for the dessert to be served a magnificent swan carved of ice and covered with a layer of sugar icing was rolled in; between its wings were peaches served on a bed of vanilla ice cream. So was born the *pêche Melba,* or peach Melba.

Later, Escoffier refined the peach Melba by adding raspberry purée to the dish. It is customarily served in restaurants without the carved-ice swan. At better hotels and restaurants throughout the world, one can still procure the original version for an extra $100 or so.

APRICOT ICE CREAM

2 cups of heavy cream
8 egg yolks
2 thin slices of lemon rind
4 tablespoons of sugar
1-1/2 cups of apricot preserves, page 115

Combine the cream, egg yolks and lemon rind in the top of a double boiler. Cook over gently boiling water, stirring constantly, until the mixture thickens and will coat a spoon. Remove this from the heat and stir in the sugar. Discard the lemon rind, cover the custard and let it cool. Uncover the preserves and place the jars in a saucepan of water over low heat until the preserves are melted but not hot. When the custard has cooled, stir in the preserves, mixing thoroughly. Pour into ice-cube trays and place in the freezer for about 4 hours, stirring occasionally.
Makes 6 servings.

APRICOT SAUCE

2 cups of apricot jam, page 63
1/2 cup of water
2 tablespoons of sugar
Kirsch

Put all ingredients except kirsch into a saucepan and boil gently for 5 minutes. Skim and strain, rubbing the fruit through a sieve. Return sauce to a double boiler to keep it hot. Just before serving, add kirsch to taste. Serve over ice cream.
Makes approximately 2-1/2 cups.

Variations

Proceed as above, substituting strawberry or raspberry jam or red currant jelly for the apricot jam. Or, to make orange sauce, proceed as above substituting 1-1/2 cups of orange marmalade and 1/2 cup apricot jam for the apricot jam, and flavor with curaçao.

Desserts & Sauces

ALMOND APRICOT CRÊPES FLAMBÉES

14 crêpes, following
2 cups of canned almond paste
2 tablespoons of rum or brandy
1 teaspoon of almond extract
1/2 cup of ground or grated blanched almonds
4 tablespoons of butter
1 cup of apricot jam, page 63
2 tablespoons of freshly squeezed lemon juice
1/4 cup of cognac

Preheat oven to 375°. Have crêpes ready to be filled. Mix together almond paste, rum or brandy, almond extract and almonds in a mixing bowl. Beat to a smooth paste. Spread the mixture over each crêpe. Fold crêpes in half, then in half again. Arrange crêpes in a buttered flameproof serving dish or chafing dish. Set aside. Mix together in a saucepan, the butter, apricot jam and lemon juice and heat just to a boil. Remove from heat and spoon the sauce over the crêpes. Heat crêpes in the oven about 15 minutes. Remove from oven, pour the cognac over them and ignite; bring flaming to the table. Serve immediately.
Makes 6 servings.

CRÊPES

If you don't have a basic crêpe batter recipe the following is very simple and lends itself to many types of jam fillings.

1 cup of all-purpose flour
1/4 teaspoon of salt
3 eggs
1-1/2 cups of milk

In a mixing bowl, sift flour and salt; add eggs and beat to a paste. Gradually add milk and beat until the batter is smooth. (This can be beaten with an electric hand mixer or a blender.) Cover and set batter in refrigerator until ready to use. Brush the bottom of a 6-1/2- to 7-inch crêpe pan with oil and heat over high heat. Remove pan from the stove and pour a small amount of the batter mixture, about 2 tablespoons, into the middle of the pan, tipping the pan in all directions to cover the bottom. Set the pan over medium heat and cook the crêpe on the first side about 1 minute; the bottom should be lightly browned. Flip crêpe over with a spatula and cook on second side about 30 seconds. Remove from pan and stack crêpes as you cook them.
Makes 14 crêpes.

BANANAS WITH GUAVA JELLY

A delicious, different dessert.

6 underripe bananas
1 cup of guava jelly, page 88
4 tablespoons of butter
4 ounces of shredded coconut
1-1/2 cups of heavy cream

Preheat oven to 375°. Peel the bananas and place them whole in a buttered baking dish. Dot with jelly and butter and bake for 30 to 40 minutes. While the bananas are baking, mix the coconut with the cream and chill. Remove the bananas from the oven, let cool and chill. Serve the bananas topped with the coconut cream.
Makes 6 servings.

Desserts & Sauces

BLACKBERRY JELLY COOKIES

1/4 pound of butter
1/3 cup of sugar
1 egg
1/2 teaspoon of vanilla extract
1/3 teaspoon of salt
1 cup of sifted all-purpose flour
Blackberry jelly, page 83 (or any firm jelly or jam)

Cream the butter and sugar together until smooth. Beat in the egg and vanilla. Add the salt to the flour and sift into the butter mixture. Mix well to form a dough and chill for several hours. On a floured board, roll out the dough and, with a cookie cutter, cut out 28 2-inch squares. Spread 14 of the squares lightly with blackberry jelly. Cover the jelly-spread squares with the remaining 14 squares of dough and bake on a greased cookie sheet at 375° for 10 minutes.
Makes 14 rich cookies.

ENGLISH CUMBERLAND SAUCE

Serve hot over baked or boiled ham.

2 cups of port wine
1/3 cup of freshly grated orange rind
2/3 cup of freshly squeezed orange juice
2 tablespoons of freshly squeezed lemon juice
1 cup of red currant jelly, page 85
1/2 cup of white sultana raisins
Dash of cayenne pepper

In a saucepan, combine port and orange rind; cook over medium heat about 15 minutes. Stir in orange juice, lemon juice, red currant jelly, raisins and cayenne pepper until well blended. Bring to a boil, reduce heat and simmer for about 10 minutes, or until jelly has melted and mixture is thick.
Makes about 2 cups.

JELLY ROLL

3 eggs
1 cup of sugar
1 teaspoon of vanilla extract
1/3 cup of water
1 cup of cake flour
1 teaspoon of baking powder
1/4 teaspoon of salt
1-1/4 cups of red currant jelly, page 85 (or your
    favorite jam or jelly)
Confectioner's sugar

Preheat oven to 375°. Line a 15 x 10 x 1-inch jelly roll pan with oiled waxed paper. In a small mixing bowl, beat the eggs about 5 minutes until they are thick and lemon colored. Pour eggs into a large mixing bowl and gradually beat in the granulated sugar. Mix the vanilla with the water and gradually beat it into the mixture. Combine flour, baking powder and salt and gradually beat it into the mixture until it is smooth. Pour into the jelly roll pan, spreading evenly to the corners. Bake 15 minutes, or until a wooden toothpick inserted in the center comes out clean. Sprinkle a towel generously with confectioner's sugar and invert cake onto it, carefully removing the waxed paper. While hot, roll up cake and towel from the narrow end. Cool on a wire rack. Unroll and remove the towel. Beat jelly with a fork and spread liberally over the cake. Roll up. Sprinkle with confectioner's sugar. Makes approximately 10 servings.

Desserts & Sauces

MARMALADE-HONEY SYRUP

*Serve over ice cream
or with waffles or pancakes.*

1 cup of mild honey
2 cups of orange marmalade, page 105

Place honey in a saucepan and add the marmalade. Bring slowly to a boil, stirring constantly, and serve at once.
Makes approximately 2 cups.

MARMALADE PUDDING

1 egg
1/2 cup of milk
1 cup of orange marmalade, page 105
1 cup of chopped beef suet
1 cup of white seedless raisins
2-1/2 cups of stale bread crumbs
1 teaspoon of baking soda
1 teaspoon of hot water

Beat the egg well and add the milk, mixing thoroughly. Mix in the marmalade, suet, raisins and bread crumbs. Stir the mixture thoroughly. Dissolve the baking soda in the hot water and add it to marmalade mixture. Pour this into a well-greased, 8-cup pudding mold and cover. Place on a rack in a large kettle. Pour boiling water into the kettle to half the depth of the mold. Cover and steam for 2-1/2 hours. Replenish the boiling water in the kettle from time to time, if necessary. When pudding is cooked, remove mold from kettle and invert pudding onto a platter. Serve with hard sauce or whipped cream.
Makes 8 servings.

BAKED APPLES WITH ORANGE MARMALADE SAUCE

This is a luscious hot dessert in winter or it can be served chilled with cream in the summer.

6 large, firm cooking apples
1 cup of orange marmalade, page 105

Preheat oven to 400°. Wash and core the apples and peel halfway down. Place them in a casserole, peeled side up. Heat 3/4 cup of the marmalade and pour it over the apples. Cover the casserole and bake about 25 minutes or until the fruit is tender, basting with the marmalade 4 or 5 times. When they are tender, pour the remaining marmalade over the apples, and put them under the broiler for 3 or 4 minutes.
Makes 6 servings.

Desserts & Sauces

GINGER-PEAR MARMALADE ROLL

A tantalizing treat for a dinner party.

4 eggs
1 cup of sugar
2 tablespoons of freshly squeezed orange juice
1 tablespoon of freshly grated orange rind
1 cup of cake flour
1 teaspoon of baking powder
1 teaspoon of ground ginger
1/2 teaspoon of ground cinnamon
1/4 teaspoon of salt
1/2 pint of whipping cream
1-1/4 cups of ginger-pear marmalade, page 107

Beat the eggs with an electric or manual beater for about 10 minutes, or until they are a creamy consistency. Gradually beat in the sugar, orange juice and rind. Sift the flour, baking powder, ginger, cinnamon and salt into the egg mixture and fold it in thoroughly. Pour batter into a 15 x 10 x 1-inch jelly roll pan lined with oiled waxed paper and bake the cake in a 375° oven for 15 to 17 minutes, or until it withdraws from the sides of the pan.

Turn the cake out on a board covered with 2 long overlapping sheets of waxed paper. Gently strip the paper from the bottom of the cake and roll up the cake in the waxed paper from the narrow end; let cool. One hour before dinner, unroll the cake and whip the cream. Combine the whipped cream with 3/4 cup of the ginger-pear marmalade and spread this thickly on the cake. Heat the remaining marmalade to a spreadable consistency, reroll the cake and glaze the surface with the warm marmalade.

Makes approximately 10 servings.

PEACH JAM BUN

Does this remind you
of your first baked Alaska?

2 eggs
1/3 cup of butter
1-3/4 cups of brown sugar (tightly packed)
1-2/3 cups of sifted cake flour
Salt
3/4 teaspoon of baking soda
2/3 cup of sour milk
2 cups of peach jam, page 72
1 cup of whipping cream
3/4 cup of chopped walnuts

Separate the eggs and beat the yolks, reserving the whites for meringue; set beaten yolks and the whites aside. Cream the butter and gradually add 1 cup of the sugar to the butter, mixing until very light. Beat the egg yolks into the butter mixture and set aside. Sift the flour with a pinch of salt. Dissolve the baking soda in the sour milk and add to the butter mixture alternately with the flour mixture. Pour batter into a greased 3-inch-deep pan. Bake in a 350° oven for about 30 minutes, or until a toothpick inserted in center of cake comes out clean. Remove cake from oven; let cool.

Whip the cream. Cover the cooled cake with a thick layer of peach jam, and over this a layer of whipped cream. Make a meringue by adding a pinch of salt to the egg whites and beating them until stiff. Gradually beat into the egg whites the remaining 3/4 cup of brown sugar a little at a time. Fold in the walnuts and spread meringue over the cake. Place cake under the broiler flame for 5 minutes or less to brown.
Makes 8 servings.

Desserts & Sauces

TIPSY PEACHES

6 fresh ripe peaches
1 cup of bar-le-duc, page 114
3/4 cup of brandy
1/4 pound of butter

Wash, peel, halve and pit the peaches. Fill the bottom of each half with bar-le-duc; then saturate them with brandy. Cut the butter into 12 thin slices. Cover the jelly in the center of each piece with 1 slice. Heat through under the broiler, using a low flame. Serve hot.
Makes 6 servings.

PEACH MELBA

4 large ripe peaches (1 15-ounce can of peach
    halves may be used in winter)
1 pint of vanilla ice cream
Melba sauce, following
1/2 pint of whipping cream
2 tablespoons of chopped walnuts

Wash, peel, halve and pit the peaches. Put one-fourth of the ice cream in each of 4 dessert glasses. Place 2 peach halves on top of each ice cream scoop and cover with Melba sauce. Whip the cream and place a dollop on top of each serving. Sprinkle on chopped walnuts for decoration. Serve at once.
Makes 4 servings.

MELBA SAUCE

4 tablespoons of red currant jelly, page 85
2 cups of raspberry jam, page 74
2 teaspoons of cornstarch
1 tablespoon of cold water

Mix the jelly and jam together in a saucepan and bring slowly to a boil. Blend the cornstarch with the cold water to form a smooth paste and stir in a little of the raspberry mixture. Return the cornstarch mixture to the saucepan and bring mixture to a boil again, stirring constantly with a wooden spoon until it is thick and clear. Strain and cool before using.

PLUM JAM WHIP FOR MERINGUE SHELLS

This should make you plum happy!

1/2 cup of heavy cream
1 cup of Damson plum jam, page 67
4 meringue shells, following

Whip cream, gradually folding in the plum jam. Chill for 1 hour until firm. Spoon into meringue shells and serve.
Makes 4 servings.

MERINGUE SHELLS

1 egg white
1/4 cup of sugar
Pinch of salt
1/4 teaspoon of vanilla extract
1/4 teaspoon of vinegar

Beat the egg white until stiff but not dry. Beat in half of the sugar and continue beating until the egg white holds its shape. Fold in the remaining sugar, salt, vanilla and vinegar. Shape the mixture into 4 cups with a pastry tube, or line 4 4-inch tart pans with it. Bake in a 275° oven for 1 hour, or until thoroughly dry but not browned.

This makes 4 meringue shells for the above plum jam whip. However, this recipe may be successfully doubled or quadrupled, and you will have meringues in your freezer for use with other jams.
Makes 4 meringue shells.

POACHED PEARS IN APRICOT JAM

1 cup of apricot jam, page 63
Juice of 1 lemon
1/2 cup of water
6 pears

Combine apricot jam, lemon juice and water in a large saucepan; bring to a boil. Wash, peel, core and halve the pears. Add them to the syrup and simmer very gently, turning them often until tender, about 15 minutes. Remove cooked pears and boil the syrup 5 minutes longer. Pour this syrup over the pears and chill before serving.
Makes 6 servings.

Desserts & Sauces

QUINCE NECTAR

Beautiful over hot pudding or custards.

4 pounds of quinces
3 pounds of apples
Juice of 2 medium-size oranges
6 cups of sugar (3 pounds)

Wash, peel and core the quinces and apples. Put both fruits through a meat grinder or dice them. Put the pulp into a preserving kettle with enough water to barely cover. Add the orange juice and heat to a rolling boil over high heat; then lower heat, cover and simmer for 15 minutes. Add sugar and continue cooking until the sugar has dissolved, stirring constantly. Ladle into hot, sterilized jars and seal immediately according to directions in Chapter 1.
Makes approximately 16 half-pints.

ENGLISH SHERRY TRIFLE

Delicious Christmas-season treat.

1 8-inch round sponge cake
1 cup of cream sherry
1 cup of raspberry jam, page 74
Custard sauce, following
1/2 pint of whipping cream
4 tablespoons of slivered toasted almonds
Candied green and red cherries

Split sponge cake into 2 layers. Put 1 layer into a deep glass bowl and sprinkle 1/2 cup of the sherry over it. Spread with raspberry jam. Place the other layer on top of the jam and sprinkle remaining 1/2 cup of sherry on it. Cover bowl and refrigerate for 2 hours. Remove bowl from refrigerator and cover cake with cooled custard sauce. Return cake to refrigerator and chill overnight. Whip the cream and, just before serving, spread it on top of the custard. Decorate with almonds and cherries. Makes 8 servings.

CUSTARD SAUCE

2 tablespoons of cornstarch
2 cups of milk
3 tablespoons of sugar
3 egg yolks
3 tablespoons of water

Blend cornstarch with 1/2 cup of the milk and set aside. Beat together the sugar, egg yolks and water and set aside. In a double boiler, scald remaining 1-1/2 cups of milk and very slowly add the cornstarch mixture, stirring constantly. Ladle out about 1/2 cup of the hot milk and beat the egg yolk mixture into it. Gradually return milk mixture to the double boiler, stirring constantly. Continue stirring and cook for 5 to 10 minutes to a thin custard consistency. Remove from heat and let cool.

Desserts & Sauces

RASPBERRY JAM CAKE

6 tablespoons of butter
1 cup of sugar
2 eggs
3 tablespoons of sour cream
1-1/2 cups of cake flour
1 teaspoon of baking powder
1 teaspoon of baking soda
1/2 teaspoon of ground cinnamon
1 teaspoon of ground nutmeg
2 cups of raspberry jam, page 74
1/2 cup of chopped walnuts or pecans
1/2 pint of heavy whipping cream

Preheat oven to 350°. Cream together the butter and sugar until light. Beat the eggs and add with the sour cream to the butter mixture. Sift together the flour, baking powder, baking soda, cinnamon and nutmeg. Add sifted ingredients to butter mixture, stirring until slightly blended. Add 1 cup of the raspberry jam and the nuts and mix lightly. Pour into a greased 7-inch bundt pan and bake for 30 minutes, or until cake springs back at the touch of your fingertip. Remove from oven and let cool. Whip the cream, combine it with the remaining cup of raspberry jam and cover the cooled cake with it.
Makes 8 servings.

CHRISTIE'S DANISH TORTE

2 tablespoons of butter
6 rusks
1/2 cup of sugar
1/2 teaspoon of ground cinnamon
Strawberry jam, page 75
3 eggs
1-1/2 tablespoons of cornstarch
2 cups of milk
2 tablespoons of sugar

Melt the butter and set aside. Crumb the rusks and combine them with 1/2 cup of sugar, cinnamon and melted butter. Mix thoroughly, forming a paste. Line a 9-inch pie pan with the paste, reserving a little to sprinkle on top of the torte. Spread strawberry jam liberally onto the bottom of the crust and set aside.

Separate the eggs, beat the yolks with the cornstarch and set yolk mixture and the whites aside. In a double boiler, scald the milk. Stir in the 2 tablespoons of sugar. Ladle out about 1/2 cup of the hot milk and beat the egg yolk-cornstarch mixture into it gradually. Slowly return milk mixture to pan and stir constantly until thickened. Pour custard over strawberry jam layer and set aside. Beat the reserved whites until stiff and cover the custard with them. Sprinkle top with reserved rusk paste and bake in a 250° oven for 30 to 35 minutes.
Makes 6 servings.

STRAWBERRIES EXOTICA

3 pounds of strawberries
2 cups of strawberry jam, page 75
1/4 cup of kirsch

Wash and hull the strawberries. Drain well, put in a dessert bowl and chill. Soften jam with kirsch. When ready to serve, pour the softened jam over the strawberries which have been well drained. This makes the strawberries shiny and gives them a delicious taste.
Makes 8 to 10 servings.

BREAD, BUTTER AND JAM PUDDING

Children love it; nostalgic with grown-ups.

4 slices of white bread
Butter
3/4 cup of strawberry jam, page 75
4 egg yolks
3 egg whites
Dash of ground nutmeg
1/2 cup of sugar
2 cups of warm milk
1/2 teaspoon of vanilla extract

Trim off crusts from bread slices; cut each slice in half and butter 1 side of each piece generously. Place in layers, butter side up, in a well-buttered, 1-quart baking dish, spreading strawberry jam between each layer. Beat egg yolks and egg whites together with sugar and nutmeg. Stir in warm milk and vanilla and pour mixture over layered bread slices. Let stand for 30 minutes. Bake in a 375° oven for about 45 minutes, or until pudding is set and lightly browned.
Makes 6 servings.

Desserts & Sauces

TART PASTRY

2 cups of sifted all-purpose flour
3/4 teaspoon of salt
2/3 cup of shortening
5 tablespoons of cold water

Sift flour and salt together and cut in the shortening with 2 knives. Add the water a little at a time until the mixture will hold together. Roll out the dough 1/8 inch thick and cut into rounds to fit muffin or tart pans. Lift the dough into the tart or muffin pans, leaving a 1/2-inch overhanging border. Fold the dough under and back to make an upright rim, then flute the edges. Prick the crust thoroughly with a fork and bake in a 450° oven about 15 minutes, or until delicately browned.
Makes 16 2-inch tart shells, or 12 4-inch tart shells.

GENEVIEVE'S BLUEBERRY JAM TARTS

1/4 pound of butter
1 cup of sugar
5 tablespoons of flour
3 egg yolks
1/4 cup of blueberry jam, page 66
1 teaspoon of vanilla extract
6 unbaked 4-inch tart shells (1/2 recipe of
   tart pastry, preceding)
3 egg whites
1/2 cup of sugar

Preheat oven to 400°. Cream the butter, gradually adding the 1 cup of sugar, and beat thoroughly. Add the flour and beat again. Slightly beat egg yolks and mix them with the blueberry jam and vanilla until well blended. Combine butter mixture with jam mixture, mixing thoroughly. Pour into unbaked tart shells. Bake the tarts for 15 to 20 minutes, or until filling is firm to the touch.
Beat the egg whites until stiff. Gradually beat in the 1/2 cup of sugar. Cover the tarts with this meringue. Bake at 300° until lightly browned, about 20 to 25 minutes. Cool and serve.
Makes 6 servings.

TARTLETS ST. DENIS

A dessert "distingué"!

1 recipe of tart pastry dough, preceding
1/4 pound of butter
1/2 cup of sugar
4 egg yolks
1/2 cup of ground blanched almonds
2 tablespoons of cornstarch
1/2 teaspoon of vanilla extract
2 egg whites
1/4 cup of raspberry jam, page 74

Preheat oven to 350°. Cream the butter and sugar together until thick and smooth. Beat in the egg yolks. When this is well blended, add the ground almonds, cornstarch and vanilla, mixing thoroughly. Beat the egg whites until stiff and fold into mixture. Line 12 4-inch tart pans with the pastry dough (or you may use muffin pans). Spread a teaspoon of raspberry jam at the bottom of each, and cover it with the almond mixture. Bake until golden brown, about 30 minutes.
Makes 12 servings.

CONGRESS TARTS

1/2 recipe of tart pastry dough, preceding
2/3 cup of ground blanched almonds
1/2 cup of sugar
1-1/2 tablespoons of cornstarch
1 egg
1 tablespoon of heavy cream
1/4 teaspoon of almond extract
2 tablespoons of red currant jelly, page 85
Whipped cream
Toasted whole almonds

Preheat oven to 350°. In a medium-size bowl, combine ground almonds, sugar and cornstarch, mixing well. In a small bowl, beat the egg until it is foamy. Add beaten egg, heavy cream and almond extract to almond mixture. Stir until well mixed. Line 6 4-inch tart pans with the pastry dough. Put a teaspoon of jelly in the bottom of each shell. Then spoon almond mixture evenly into the shells and bake 30 minutes until golden brown and the center springs back when pressed with fingertip. Cool on wire rack. Decorate with whipped cream and whole almonds.
Makes 6 servings.

Desserts & Sauces

KIWI TART "VICTORIANA"

1/2 recipe of pie shell pastry dough, following
Flour
1 egg yolk
Water
6 to 8 kiwi berries (fairly firm)
1 tablespoon of freshly squeezed lemon juice
1 tablespoon of sugar

Apricot Glaze

1/2 cup of apricot jam, page 63
1 tablespoon of water

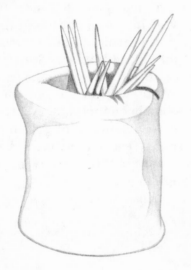

Preheat oven to 425°. Roll pastry dough out on a lightly floured board to a 12 x 5-inch rectangle. Flour lightly and fold in half to form a 12 x 2-1/2-inch rectangle. Cut a 1-inch border from the 3 unfolded sides of the rectangle and set it aside. Roll folded pastry out again to 12 x 5 inches and put it on a baking tray. Lightly beat the egg yolk with a little water and brush the edges of the pastry with some of the mixture. Unfold the 1-inch strip, which now makes a rectangular frame, and place it on top of the pastry to form a border. Trim evenly. Prick the bottom of the pastry and, using a knife, make crisscrosses on the border. Wash, peel and slice the kiwi berries. Arrange rows of overlapping kiwi slices down the center of the pastry. Sprinkle lemon juice and sift sugar over the fruit. Brush any sugar off the pastry, and lightly brush pastry with remaining egg yolk mixture. Bake for 20 to 30 minutes. While tart is baking, make apricot glaze by heating apricot jam and water together until well blended. Pass mixture through a wire sieve, return to pan and bring to a boil. Boil gently until the glaze is clear and of a spreadable consistency. Remove tart from oven and while still hot, brush kiwi slices with the glaze. Makes 6 servings.

PIE SHELL PASTRY

2 cups of sifted all-purpose flour
3/4 teaspoon of salt
1/3 cup of shortening
2-1/2 tablespoons of cold water

Sift the flour and salt together and cut in the shortening with 2 knives or a pastry cutter. Add the water, a little at a time, until the mixture will hold together. Divide the dough in half. Roll out one-half of the dough 1/8 inch thick on a floured board to fit a 9-inch pie pan. Lift the dough into the pie pan, being careful not to stretch it. After the dough is fitted, trim the edges evenly, leaving a 1-inch overhanging border. Fold the border under and back to make an upright rim. Then flute the edges. Repeat this process with the remaining half of the dough. Prick the crusts thoroughly with a fork and bake for 15 minutes in a preheated 450° oven. (If you wish to make only 1 crust, half of the dough may be frozen for later use.)
Makes 2 9-inch pie shells.

MARMALADE PIES

1 recipe of pie shell pastry dough, preceding
3/4 cup of orange marmalade, page 105
Milk
Sugar

Preheat oven to 400°. Divide pastry dough into 8 equal parts. Roll each part into a 5-inch circle on a floured surface. Spread 1-1/2 tablespoons of marmalade on one-half of each circle, leaving a 1/2-inch edge. Moisten edge of circle with water, fold over marmalade-covered half and press edges together with the tines of a fork. Brush tops with milk, sprinkle with sugar and place on an ungreased baking sheet. Bake 20 minutes, or until golden brown. Remove from oven and cool on wire rack. Cool slightly and serve warm.
Makes 8 servings.

The Elysium of John Evelyn

CZAR PETER the Great of Russia may have been a great favorite of England's King William of Orange, but to John Evelyn he was a monster. That diarist and distinguished public official was a dedicated gardener. Upon being granted the crown property of Sayes Court, Deptford, Evelyn, over a period of years, transformed a run-down orchard and 100 barren acres into a marvel of gardens, walks, groves and enclosures. It was a formal, stylized garden, for Evelyn preferred nature tamed and trimmed to nature free style. The pride of the garden was a hedge of holly, five feet high.

Evelyn was at the family home at Wotton in Surrey when Peter the Great came to England to study shipbuilding at Deptford. King William installed the Czar at Sayes Court, so that he could be near the shipways. John Evelyn first learned things went badly from a servant at the house who wrote, "There is a house full of people, and right nasty. The Czar lies next your library, and dines in the parlour next your study. He dines at 10 o'clock and 6 at night, is very seldom at home a whole day, very often in the King's Yard, or by water, dressed in several dresses." In boisterous moods the Czar did great damage to the lawns, the fruit trees and the bowling green, and his favorite morning exercise was to have a servant push him in a wheelbarrow through Evelyn's prized holly hedge. After Peter the Great departed, Sir Christopher Wren and the King's gardener estimated the damage to the property at 321 pounds. In his book, *Sylva,* Evelyn sadly reflects "on my now ruined garden, thanks to the Czar of Muscovy."

Sylva was the answer to inquiries by the Commissioners of the Navy to the Royal Society, of which Evelyn was a founder, regarding the future supply of timber for shipbuilding. Evelyn prepared a detailed paper presented to the society in 1662; an expanded version was printed as *Sylva* two years later. He advocated changes in forestry practices to correct the wasteful methods being used. His recommendations were generally adopted, and did much to halt "the notorious decay" of England's "wooden walls." Disraeli spoke the truth when he said Lord Nelson's fleets were built from the oaks that Evelyn had planted.

John Evelyn was a man of wide-ranging interests—mathematics, chemistry, anatomy, astronomy, shipping, numismatics, the graphic arts, building and planting. He was a friend of kings, yet a man who refused to accept a title. He inscribed to King Charles II his *Fumifugium; or, the Inconvenience of the Air and Smoke of London Dissipated.* Although he proposed some ingenious solutions, the results were not as satisfying as those of *Sylva.* It was not until the killer smogs of post-World War II that the London air was effectively scrubbed.

Evelyn's taste for the formal garden is nowhere better shown than in his account of the gardens of Cardinal Richelieu's villa at Rueil. He speaks of the "walks" of vast length. "On one of these walks, within a square of tall trees, is a basilisk of copper, which, managed by the fountaineer, casts water nearly sixty feet high, and will of itself move around so swiftly, that one can hardly escape wetting. This leads to the Citronière, which is a noble conserve of all those rarities; and at the end of it the Arch of Constantine, painted on a wall in oil, as large as the real one at Rome, so well done, that even a man skilled in painting may mistake it for stone and sculpture. The sky and hills, which seem to be between the arches, are so natural, that swallows and other birds, thinking to fly through, have dashed themselves against the wall. I was infinitely taken with this agreeable cheat."

He speaks of artificial waterfalls, of ponds with moss and ivy-covered islands, properly shaded, so that fowl may breed and lay eggs. "We then saw a large and very rare grotto of shellwork, in the shape of satyrs and other fancies; in the middle stands a marble table, on which a fountain plays in divers forms of glasses, cups, crosses, fans, crowns, etc."

John Evelyn's lifelong project was the compilation of a vast *Elysium Brittanicum,* or *Cyclopedia of Horticulture.* Samuel Pepys refers to it in his *Diary.* "By water to Deptford, and there made a visit to Mr. Evelyn. . . . He read to me very much also of his discourse, he hath been many years and now is about, about Gardenage; which will be a most noble and pleasant piece." Although Evelyn lived to be 86, under six regimes from Charles I to Queen Anne, public demands upon his talents precluded completion of so ambitious a project. "Minding his books and his garden" was an unfulfilled wish. It is probable that a completed *Elysium Brittanicum* would have contained *Sylva, Aceteria,* and *Kalendarium Hortense.*

Aceteria, or a Book of Sallets, was the last published work of Evelyn. It combines recipes with descriptions of the fruits and vegetables that make an agreeable salad. From this work, originally published in 1699, we come upon these paragraphs on the melon.

"Melon, *Melo;* to have been reckon'd rather among *Fruits;* and tho' an usual Ingredient in our *Sallet;* yet for its transcendent delicacy and flavor, cooling and exhilirating Nature (if sweet, dry, weighty and well-fed) not only superior to the *Gourd*-kind, but Paragon with the noblest Productions of the Garden. *Jos. Scaliger* and *Casaubon,* think our *Melon* unknown to the Ancients, (which others contradict) as yet under the name of *Cucumers:* But he who reads how artificially they were Cultivated, rais'd under Glasses, and expos'd to the hot Sun, (for *Tiberius*) cannot well doubt of their being the same with ours.

"There is also a *Winter-Melon,* large and with black Seeds, exceedingly Cooling, brought us from abroad, and the hotter Climates, where they drink *Water* after eating *Melons;* but in the colder (after all dispute) *Wine* is judg'd the better: That it has indeed by some been accus'd as apt to corrupt in the Stomach (as do all things else eaten in excess) is not deny'd: But a perfect good *Melon* is certainly as harmless a Fruit as any whatsoever; and may safely be mingl'd with *Sallet,* in Pulp or Slices, or more properly eaten by it self, with a little *Salt* and *Pepper;* for a *Melon* which requires *Sugar* to commend it, wants of Perfection. *Note,* That this Fruit was very rarely cultivated in *England,* so as to bring it to Maturity, till Sir *Geo. Gardner* came out of Spain. I my self remembring, when an ordinary *Melon* would have sold for five or six Shillings. The small unripe Fruit, when the others are past, may be Pickl'd with *Mango,* and are very delicate."

XI Pickles & Relishes

Almost anything may be pickled, from nasturtium seeds to walnuts. One of the primary keys to success in pickling is freshness. Select firm, tender vegetables and fruits at the height of their season for best flavor and highest food value. Keep in mind the local farmers' market, the stands that have recently sprung up on the outskirts of our cities, or nearby farms (where you may even be able to pick the produce yourself) for buying your fruits and vegetables. These places offer in-season produce that will be both fresher and less expensive than you would find at your local supermarket.

Try to use any fruits or vegetables within 24 hours of picking, or immediately after buying, and keep them in a cool place until you are ready to begin the pickling process. Use only unwaxed cucumbers for pickling with their skins on, because the brine cannot penetrate the wax.

It is tremendously rewarding to set out on your table pickles and relishes you have preserved for out-of-season use. You will never regret the money and labor that have gone into preparing this bounty. The following recipes for pickles and relishes are quick and easy, and never become a "major project" in the kitchen.

TYPES OF PICKLES AND RELISHES

SOUR PICKLES

Made from vegetables or fruits, these are not necessarily cooked. Sour pickles are first brined, which removes excess water, and are then preserved in spiced vinegar. Consequently, the vinegar acts as a preservative because it has not been diluted with excess water.

SWEET PICKLES

These are cooked vegetables and fruits, usually making brining unnecessary.

FRUIT PICKLES

Most often prepared from whole fruits, these pickles are simmered in a sweet, spicy syrup.

RELISHES

A mixture of chunky-cut fruits or vegetables, a relish may be sweet and sour in flavor or savory spiced.

CATSUP

This is a thick sauce, mainly the product of a single vegetable or fruit that is cooked with vinegar and spices and sieved until smooth.

INGREDIENTS AND BASICS OF PICKLING

VINEGAR

Use a high-grade vinegar with 5 to 6 percent acidity; read the bottle label for the percentage before buying. Distilled white vinegar preserves the color of foods, so use it in the following recipes unless another vinegar is specified. Cider vinegar tends to darken pickles, but does give a mellow acid taste. Avoid homemade vinegars, as they may not have the required percentage of acidity. Long boiling is another way to lose acidity, which is the most important part of preserving pickles. Never reduce the amount of vinegar called for in a recipe; add sugar if the pickle is too tart.

SALT

Use only plain, pure salt, coarsely or finely ground and without additives. Canning or pickling salt is available at your local supermarket in four-pound boxes and is ideal. Do not use iodized salt, as it tends to darken pickles, or table salt, as the additives used to keep it from caking make pickling liquids cloudy.

SUGAR

Use only granulated white sugar unless the recipes calls for brown sugar, which will darken the pickles. Brown sugar is used mostly for chutneys and relishes.

HERBS AND SPICES

Use herbs and spices that have not sat too long on the shelf and lost their pungency. Keep them in airtight containers in a cool place, as they lose their strength if subjected to heat and humidity. After peeling garlic cloves, blanch the cloves for two minutes to kill any bacteria before adding them to the pickles.

LIME AND ALUM

These are not recommended to crisp pickles. Just a touch too much alum may make the pickles bitter. An old-fashioned way of crisping cucumbers is to layer them during brining with well-washed grape or cherry leaves that have not been sprayed with pesticide. Don't forget to discard the leaves before going on to the next step.

WATER

Use a good-quality drinking water. Do not use water with a high-iron content, as it will darken the pickles. If you do not have good soft water in your area, boil your tap water for 15 minutes and let it stand for 24 hours. Skim off the film that forms on the surface and ladle the water into the preserving kettle or bowl to be used. (Ladling will not disturb the sediment that has collected on the bottom of the pot.) Now add one tablespoon of vinegar to each gallon of water.

CONTAINERS AND UTENSILS

Use only stoneware crocks or glass, stainless steel, enamelware or aluminum containers for brining. Do not use any container that is chipped or cracked, made of wood or any other kind of metal, or crocks that are foreign made and perhaps inadequately glazed (the exceptions to the warning against foreign-made crocks are those from England and France). Do not use wood covers for brining; a glass cover or a dinner plate should be used. Use only stainless-steel, heavy-aluminum or unchipped enamelware preserving kettles and saucepans. Do not use cast-iron, brass, galvanized or copper kettles or pans. Cast iron darkens pickles, brass, galvanized and copper containers tend to give a metallic taste, and the acids and salts in copper cause a slightly harmful effect. Use long-handled stainless-steel or wooden spoons for stirring, and stainless-steel or enamelware slotted spoons and ladles for lifting out vegetables and fruits. Measuring cups should be made of glass.

JARS: HOW TO STERILIZE AND PACK

See Chapter 1 for information on sterilizing and head room space. Use wide-mouthed jars for packing pickles and spiced fruits. Allow 1/2-inch head room space (rather than the 1/4 inch recommended for jams and jellies) unless otherwise specified.

PROCESSING IN A WATER BATH

It is recommended today that all pickles be processed in a hot water bath. Open-kettle canning is no longer considered safe for canning pickles and relishes, as there is a danger of bacteria entering the food when it is transferred from the preserving kettle to the jar. Wild yeasts and molds, although harmless when airborne, may start to grow in the jar of unprocessed pickles.

Pack pickled products into glass jars and arrange in a water bath according to directions in Chapter 1. Once the water reaches a full boil, begin to count the processing time, which is given at the end of each pickle, relish and catsup recipe. When the jars have been removed from the bath and cooled, check for airtight seals. If the seal is not good, eat the jar's contents right away. Do not attempt to reprocess and rejar the contents.

STORING

Label each jar, including the date, and store in a cool, dark, dry place. The pickles and relishes are ready to eat about two weeks after being made, when the flavors will have mellowed, and can be kept until next season's produce is ready for putting up. Keep open jars in the refrigerator and be sure that the pickles are always covered with liquid.

PROBLEMS

Destroy completely any pickles or relishes that have a disagreeable smell or are moldy, mushy, slippery or gassy when opened. Do not taste the jar's contents to see if it has spoiled. Be on the lookout for bulging lids, leakage or broken seals; discard the contents of any jar with these defects.

Pickles & Relishes

DILL PICKLES

4 pounds of pickling cucumbers (4 inches)
8 heads of fresh dill
8 cloves of garlic
24 whole black peppercorns
2 cups of cider vinegar
4-1/2 cups of water
1/3 cup of salt

Wash the cucumbers and cut off stem and blossom ends, but do not peel. Wash the heads of dill and peel and blanch the garlic. Have 8 pint-size hot, sterilized jars ready. Put 1 dill head, 3 peppercorns and 1 clove of garlic into the bottom of each jar. Pack the cucumbers into the jars. Combine the vinegar, water and salt in a large saucepan and bring to a boil. Ladle the solution into the jars to cover the cucumbers. Seal immediately according to directions in Chapter 1. Process in a water bath 10 minutes.
Makes approximately 8 pints.

BREAD AND BUTTER PICKLES

Everybody's favorite.

6 medium-size cucumbers
3 medium-size onions
3/4 cup of salt
4 cups of water
1 cup of vinegar
1 cup of sugar
1 teaspoon of whole mustard seeds
1 teaspoon of celery seeds
3/4 teaspoon of turmeric
1/2 teaspoon of ground ginger
1/4 teaspoon of freshly ground black pepper

Wash the cucumbers and cut off stem and blossom ends, but do not peel. Slice the cucumbers 1/4 inch thick and place in a large glass bowl. Peel and slice the onions and add them to the bowl. Combine the salt and water and pour over the vegetables. Let stand in a cool place for 3 hours. Drain the vegetables through a sieve and rinse under cold running water. Combine the vinegar, sugar, mustard seeds, celery seeds, turmeric, ginger and pepper in a preserving kettle and bring to a boil, stirring. Add the drained vegetables and simmer, uncovered, for 15 minutes, stirring occasionally. Ladle into hot, sterilized jars and seal immediately according to directions in Chapter 1. Process in a water bath 5 minutes.
Makes approximately 5 half-pints.

MUSTARD PICKLES

36 pickling cucumbers (2-1/2 inches)
1 small head of cauliflower
3 medium-size sweet green peppers
3 medium-size sweet red peppers
6 medium-size green tomatoes
1-1/2 pounds of small white onions
   (not more than 1 inch in diameter)
1 cup of salt
4 quarts of water
1-1/2 cups of sugar
1/2 cup of all-purpose flour
1 tablespoon of turmeric
1/2 cup of water
1/2 cup of prepared mustard
5 cups of vinegar

Wash the cucumbers and cut off stem and blossom ends, but do not peel. Slice the cucumbers 1/2 inch thick. Wash the cauliflower and cut into 1-inch pieces. Wash the green and red peppers, remove the seeds and membranes and cut peppers into 1/2-inch pieces. Wash, blanch, peel and chop the tomatoes. Peel the onions. Put all of the vegetables in a large glass bowl. Combine the salt and 4 quarts of water and pour over the vegetables. Let stand in a cool place for about 16 hours. Combine the sugar, flour and turmeric in a preserving kettle and slowly add the 1/2 cup of water, stirring until smooth. Now add the mustard and vinegar, bring to a boil and cook rapidly until the sauce is thick and coats a spoon, about 5 minutes. Drain the vegetables through a sieve and rinse under cold running water. Add the vegetables to the preserving kettle and simmer, uncovered, for 15 minutes. Ladle into hot, sterilized jars and seal immediately according to directions in Chapter 1. Process in a water bath 15 minutes.
Makes approximately 8 pints.

Pickles & Relishes

SWEET ICICLE PICKLES

20 cucumbers (6 inches)
1 cup of salt
9 cups of water
5 cups of sugar (2-1/2 pounds)
5 cups of vinegar
1-1/2 tablespoons of mixed whole pickling spices

Wash the cucumbers and cut off stem and blossom ends, but do not peel. Cut cucumbers into quarters lengthwise and place in a large glass bowl. Combine the salt and water in a saucepan and bring to a boil. Pour over the cucumbers and cover with a glass pie plate. Fill a glass jar with water and place on plate to hold the cucumbers submerged in the brine solution. Cover the whole bowl with a towel secured in place with twine and set in a cool place. Leave for 1 week, removing scum each day if it forms on the surface. Then drain the cucumbers through a sieve and rinse thoroughly with cold running water. Return the cucumbers to the glass bowl, cover with boiling water and let stand for 1 day. Drain the cucumbers and return them to the glass bowl. Combine the sugar and vinegar in a large saucepan. Put the pickling spices in a cheesecloth bag, add to pan, and bring to a boil, stirring. Pour the syrup over the cucumbers and let stand in a cool place for 1 day. Drain off the syrup, return to kettle, bring to a boil, and pour over cucumbers again. Repeat this procedure for 4 days. Pack the cucumbers in hot, sterilized jars. Discard the cheesecloth bag, bring the syrup to a boil and ladle the syrup over the cucumbers to cover, leaving 1/4-inch head room. Seal immediately according to directions in Chapter 1. Process in a water bath 10 minutes.
Makes approximately 6 pints.

SWEET DILL PICKLES

Unbeatable.

4 pounds of pickling cucumbers (4 inches)
3 medium-size onions
16 heads of fresh dill
6 cups of cider vinegar
6 cups of sugar (3 pounds)
6 tablespoons of salt
2 teaspoons of celery seeds
2 teaspoons of whole mustard seeds

Wash the cucumbers and cut off stem and blossom ends, but do not peel. Slice the cucumbers 1/4 inch thick. Peel and thinly slice the onions, making 32 slices in all. Wash the heads of dill. Have 8 pint-size hot, sterilized jars ready. Put 3 slices of onion and 1 dill head into the bottom of each jar. Pack the cucumber slices into the jars, leaving 1-1/2-inches head room, and place 1 onion slice and 1 dill head on top of each jar. Combine the vinegar, sugar, salt, celery seeds and mustard seeds in a large saucepan and bring to a boil, stirring. Ladle the solution into the jars to cover the cucumbers, leaving 1/4-inch head room. Seal immediately according to directions in Chapter 1. Process in a water bath 10 minutes.
Makes approximately 8 pints.

DILLED GREEN BEANS

Add zest to salads.

4 pounds of tender green snap beans
8 cloves of garlic
2 teaspoons of crushed, dried red chili pepper
4 teaspoons of whole mustard seeds
8 teaspoons of dill seeds, or 8 heads of fresh dill
5 cups of vinegar
5 cups of water
1/2 cup of salt

Wash the green beans, remove tops and tails and cut into uniform lengths to fit in pint jars. Peel and blanch the garlic. Pack the green beans in 8 pint-sized hot, sterilized jars. Put 1/4 teaspoon of red pepper, 1/2 teaspoon of whole mustard seeds, 1 teaspoon of dill seeds (or 1 head of fresh dill, well washed) and 1 garlic clove in each jar. Combine the vinegar, water and salt in a large saucepan and bring to a boil. Ladle the solution over the beans, leaving 1/4-inch head room. Seal immediately according to directions in Chapter 1. Process in a water bath 10 minutes.
Makes approximately 8 pints.

Pickles & Relishes

PICKLED BEETS

Excellent with cold cuts.

2 pounds of small beets
1 lemon
2 cups of cider vinegar
2 cups of water
2 cups of sugar (1 pound)
1 tablespoon of ground cinnamon
1 teaspoon of ground cloves
1 teaspoon of ground allspice
2 tablespoons of grated horseradish

    Wash the beets, place in a saucepan, cover with water and bring to a boil. Lower the heat and simmer until just tender. Drain the beets, dip in cold water and peel off the skins. Cut the lemon into thin slices and remove the seeds. Combine the lemon slices, vinegar, water, sugar, cinnamon, cloves and allspice in a preserving kettle and bring to a boil, stirring. Add the whole beets and simmer for 15 minutes. Stir in the horseradish. Remove the beets with a slotted spoon and pack into hot, sterilized jars. Ladle the hot liquid into the jars to cover the beets. Seal immediately according to directions in Chapter 1. Process in a water bath 30 minutes.
Makes approximately 5 pints.

PICKLED CARROTS

Good on a relish dish.

2 pounds of uniform-size small carrots
3 cups of vinegar
1 cup of water
1 cup of sugar
3 tablespoons of mixed whole pickling spices

    Wash the carrots, place in a saucepan, cover with water and bring to a boil. Boil rapidly until half tender, about 5 minutes. Drain the carrots and peel off the skins. Combine the vinegar, water and sugar in a preserving kettle. Put the pickling spices in a cheesecloth bag, add to kettle, bring to a boil, stirring, and boil for 15 minutes. Remove the spice bag and discard it. Add the carrots to the kettle and boil until nearly tender, about 5 minutes. Remove the carrots with a slotted spoon and pack into hot, sterilized jars. Ladle the hot liquid into the jars to cover the carrots. Seal immediately according to directions in Chapter 1. Process in a water bath 30 minutes.
Makes approximately 2 pints.

MUSTARD PICKLED CAULIFLOWER

Adds zest to halibut.

2 medium-size heads of cauliflower
1/2 cup of salt
2 cups of vinegar
2 cups of sugar
1/3 cup of all-purpose flour
2 tablespoons of dry mustard
2 teaspoons of turmeric
1-1/2 teaspoons of celery seeds
1/2 cup of pimiento strips

Break cauliflowers into flowerets and wash. Place in a large glass bowl, sprinkle with the salt and add cold water to cover. Let stand in a cool place overnight. The next morning, drain the cauliflowerets through a sieve and rinse under cold running water. Combine the vinegar, sugar, flour, dry mustard, turmeric and celery seeds in a preserving kettle and bring to a boil, stirring. Add the cauliflowerets and simmer over medium heat for 5 minutes. Stir in pimiento strips and simmer 1 more minute. Remove the cauliflowerets and pimiento strips with a slotted spoon and pack into hot, sterilized jars. Boil the syrup in the kettle for about 6 minutes, stirring constantly, then ladle into the jars to cover the cauliflower. Seal immediately according to directions in Chapter 1. Process in a water bath 10 minutes.

Makes approximately 5 half-pints.

Pickles & Relishes

PICKLED ONIONS

A ploughman's lunch with cheese.

2 pounds of small white onions
   (not more than 1 inch in diameter)
1/3 cup of salt
2/3 cup of water
2 cups of vinegar
1/3 cup of sugar
1 tablespoon of mixed whole pickling spices

Place the onions in a large glass bowl and cover with boiling water. Let stand for 15 minutes. Drain and peel the onions and return them to the bowl. Sprinkle the onions with the salt and add cold water to cover. Cover the bowl with an inverted glass plate and let stand for 48 hours. Drain the onions through a sieve and rinse under cold running water. Combine the water, vinegar, and sugar in a preserving kettle. Put the pickling spices in a cheesecloth bag, add to kettle and bring to a boil, stirring. Add the onions to the kettle and boil for 5 minutes. Remove the spice bag and discard it. Remove the onions with a slotted spoon and pack into hot, sterilized jars. Ladle the hot liquid into the jars to cover the onions. Seal immediately according to directions in Chapter 1. Process in a water bath 5 minutes.
Makes approximately 2 pints.

PICKLED ZUCCHINI

2 pounds of firm zucchini
2 medium-size onions
1/4 cup of salt
2 cups of sugar (1 pound)
2-1/2 cups of cider vinegar
2 teaspoons of whole mustard seeds
1 teaspoon of celery seeds
1 teaspoon of turmeric

Wash the zucchini and cut off stem and blossom ends, but do not peel. Slice the zucchini 1/4 inch thick. Peel and quarter the onions and cut in thin slices. Place the zucchini and onions in a large glass bowl, sprinkle with salt and add cold water to cover. Let stand in a cool place for 2 hours. Drain the vegetables through a sieve, rinse under cold running water and return to the bowl. Combine the sugar, vinegar, mustard seeds, celery seeds and turmeric in a preserving kettle and bring to a boil. Pour the hot liquid over the vegetables and let stand for 2 hours. Put the vegetable mixture in the preserving kettle, bring to a boil and boil for 5 minutes. Ladle into hot, sterilized jars and seal immediately according to directions in Chapter 1. Process in a water bath 15 minutes.
Makes approximately 3 pints.

CANTALOUPE PICKLES

1 large cantaloupe
4 cups of cider vinegar
2 cups of water
1 teaspoon of ground mace
2 3-inch sticks of cinnamon
2 tablespoons of whole cloves
4 cups of sugar (2 pounds)

Wash, peel and seed the cantaloupe. Cut the cantaloupe into 1-inch cubes and place in a large glass bowl. Combine the vinegar, water and mace in a large saucepan. Put the cinnamon and cloves in a cheesecloth bag, add to saucepan and bring to a boil. Pour the solution over the cantaloupe and let stand in a cool place overnight. Drain the cantaloupe through a sieve, reserving the liquid. Place the liquid in a preserving kettle, bring to a boil and stir in the sugar. Add the cantaloupe and simmer, uncovered, until transparent, about 1 hour. Remove the spice bag and discard it. Remove the cantaloupe with a slotted spoon and pack into hot, sterilized jars. Bring liquid to a boil and boil 10 minutes. Ladle the hot syrup into the jars to cover the cantaloupe, leaving 1/4-inch head room. Seal immediately according to directions in Chapter 1. Process in a water bath 5 minutes.
Makes approximately 2 pints.

PICKLED CRAB APPLES

Good accompaniment to pork.

4 pounds of uniform-size crab apples
4 cups of cider vinegar
4 cups of sugar (2 pounds)
6 2-inch sticks of cinnamon
1 tablespoon of whole allspice
1 tablespoon of whole cloves
1/2 teaspoon of whole mace

Wash the crab apples but do not pare. Combine the vinegar and sugar in a preserving kettle. Put the cinnamon, allspice, cloves, and mace in a cheesecloth bag, add to kettle and bring to boil, stirring. Simmer syrup for 8 minutes. Turn off heat and let syrup cool. Add the crab apples to kettle, bring slowly to a boil and simmer for 10 minutes; be careful not to let the fruit burst. Remove the kettle from the heat and let the fruit stand in the syrup in a cool place overnight. Remove the spice bag and discard it. Remove the crab apples with a slotted spoon and pack into hot, sterilized jars. Bring the syrup to a boil and ladle into the jars to cover the crab apples. Seal immediately according to directions in Chapter 1. Process in a water bath 15 minutes.
Makes approximately 5 pints.

Pickles & Relishes

FIG PICKLES

8 pounds of firm ripe figs
2 quarts of water
1 tablespoon of salt
8 cups of brown sugar (tightly packed)
4 cups of vinegar
2 teaspoons of whole cloves
6 3-inch sticks of cinnamon

Wash the figs. Combine the water, salt and figs in a preserving kettle, bring to a boil and simmer for 15 minutes. Drain the figs through a sieve and rinse under cold running water. Combine the sugar and vinegar in a preserving kettle. Put the cloves and cinnamon in a cheesecloth bag, add to kettle and bring to a boil, stirring. Add the figs and simmer, uncovered, for 1 hour. Remove the figs with a slotted spoon and pack into hot, sterilized jars. Ladle the hot syrup over to cover the figs, leaving 1/4-inch head room. Seal immediately according to directions in Chapter 1. Process in a water bath 15 minutes.
Makes approximately 8 pints.

PAUL'S PICKLED PINEAPPLE

A "must" with pork or ham.

1 large pineapple
2 cups of sugar (1 pound)
2 cups of water
1 cup of vinegar
1 teaspoon of salt
1 2-inch stick of cinnamon
4 whole cloves

Wash and peel the pineapple. Cut the pineapple crosswise into 1-inch-thick slices. Cut the core from the pineapple slices and discard. Dice the slices into 1-inch squares. Combine the sugar and water in a preserving kettle and bring to a boil, stirring. Add the pineapple pieces to the kettle and boil for about 10 minutes. Remove the pineapple with a slotted spoon and set aside. Add the vinegar, salt, cinnamon and cloves to the kettle and boil the syrup until thickened, about 15 minutes. Place the pineapple back in the syrup and boil for about 5 minutes. Ladle into hot, sterilized jars and seal immediately according to directions in Chapter 1. Process in a water bath 20 minutes.
Makes approximately 3 pints.

PICKLED PEACHES

Delicious with ham.

4 pounds of ripe peaches (approximately
   2 inches in diameter)
1-1/2 tablespoons of whole cloves
Solution to prevent darkening: 2 tablespoons of salt,
   2 tablespoons of vinegar and 2 quarts of water
4 cups of sugar (2 pounds)
3/4 cup of water
1-1/2 cups of cider vinegar
Piece of ginger root the size of a walnut
2 3-inch sticks of cinnamon

Wash, blanch and peel the peaches and stud each with 2 cloves. To prevent the peaches from darkening, combine the solution ingredients in a large glass bowl and place the peaches in it. Combine the sugar, water and vinegar in a preserving kettle. Put the ginger, remaining cloves and cinnamon in a cheesecloth bag, add to kettle and bring to a boil, stirring. Drain the peaches through a sieve and rinse under cold running water. Cook half of the peaches in the simmering syrup for 10 minutes. Remove the peaches with a slotted spoon and place in a large glass bowl. Now cook the remaining peaches for 10 minutes, remove and add to the bowl. Pour the hot syrup over the peaches. Let stand to plump in a cool place overnight. The next morning, remove the peaches from the syrup with a slotted spoon and pack into hot, sterilized jars. Bring the syrup to a boil in a large saucepan. Remove the spice bag and discard it. Ladle the hot syrup into the jars to cover the peaches, leaving 1/4-inch head room. Seal immediately according to directions in Chapter 1. Process in a water bath 20 minutes.
Makes approximately 4 pints.

Pickles & Relishes

SPICED FRUIT PICKLE

Delicious with domestic fowl.

5 firm peaches
3 firm pears
1 large onion
9 ripe tomatoes
10 stalks of celery
1 sweet red pepper
1 sweet green pepper
1 tablespoon of mixed whole pickling spices
1 dried red chili pepper
2-1/2 cups of sugar (1-1/4 pounds)
1 cup of vinegar
1 tablespoon of salt

Wash, blanch, peel and pit the peaches. Cut the peaches into small pieces. Peel, core and chop the pears. Peel and chop the onion. Wash, blanch, and peel the tomatoes and cut into small pieces. Wash and chop the celery stalks. Wash the sweet peppers, remove seeds and membranes and chop. Put all of the vegetables in a preserving kettle. Put the pickling spices in a cheesecloth bag and add to kettle, together with chili pepper, sugar, vinegar and salt. Bring to a boil, stirring. Lower the heat and simmer, uncovered, for 2 hours, or until mixture thickens. Remove chili pepper and spice bag and discard them. Ladle into hot, sterilized jars and seal immediately according to directions in Chapter 1. Process in a water bath 20 minutes.
Makes approximately 4 pints.

WATERMELON RIND PICKLES

1 large watermelon (about 6 pounds)
2 quarts of water
3/4 cup of salt
1 lemon
8 cups of cider vinegar
9 cups of sugar (4-1/2 pounds)
2 pieces of ginger root the size of a walnut
3 3-inch sticks of cinnamon
2 tablespoons of whole cloves

Trim the green skin and pink pulp from the watermelon rind. Cut the rind into 1-inch cubes and put into a large glass bowl. Combine the water and salt and pour over the rind. Let stand in a cool place for 8 hours. Drain the rind through a sieve and rinse under cold running water. Put the rind in a preserving kettle, add water to cover, bring to a boil and cook until tender when pierced with a fork, about 10 minutes. Drain the rind through a sieve and set aside. Wash and thinly slice the lemon and remove the seeds. Combine the vinegar, sugar and lemon slices in a preserving kettle. Put the ginger root, cinnamon and cloves in a cheesecloth bag and add to kettle. Bring to a boil, stirring, and boil for 5 minutes. Lower the heat, add the rind and simmer, uncovered, for about 1 hour. Remove the spice bag and discard it. Ladle into hot, sterilized jars and seal immediately according to directions in Chapter 1. Process in a water bath 5 minutes.
Makes approximately 7 pints.

PICKLED WALNUTS

A gourmet treat.

100 green walnuts
3 cups of salt
2-1/2 cups of vinegar
2 tablespoons of ground allspice
1/4 cup of whole black peppercorns
1 2-inch piece of ginger root

Procure the walnuts when they are young (beginning to middle of July); be careful they are not woody. Prick the entire surface of the walnuts with the tines of a fork and put them in a large glass bowl. Sprinkle the walnuts with 1 cup of salt and add cold water to cover. Let stand in a cool place for 3 days. Drain the walnuts through a sieve and return them to the bowl. Sprinkle with 1 cup of salt and add water to cover. Let stand for another 3 days. Repeat this process one more time with remaining cup of salt. Now drain the walnuts through a sieve and spread on a tray. Place the tray in the sun for 2 or 3 days until the walnuts are perfectly black. Pack the walnuts into hot, sterilized jars about three-quarters full. Combine the vinegar, allspice and peppercorns in a large saucepan. Bruise the ginger and add to the pan. Bring to a boil and boil for 15 minutes. Ladle the solution into the jars to cover the walnuts. Seal immediately according to directions in Chapter 1.
Makes approximately 4 pints.

PICKLED EGGS

Good as an hors d'oeuvre.

6 eggs
6 cloves of garlic
2 cups of cider vinegar
1 tablespoon of mixed whole pickling spices
1 teaspoon of minced orange rind
1 teaspoon of ground mace
1 teaspoon of salt

Hard cook the eggs, peel and put in a sterilized quart jar. Peel and blanch the garlic. Combine the garlic, vinegar, pickling spices, orange rind, mace, and salt in a large saucepan, bring to a boil and boil for 10 minutes. Ladle the solution over eggs, let cool and seal with an airtight cap. Refrigerate for at least 2 days before using. The eggs can be stored in the refrigerator for up to 6 weeks.
Makes 1 quart.

Pickles & Relishes

PICCALILLI

Child's delight with hot dogs.

2 pounds of green tomatoes
1 small head of cabbage
2 large onions
2 large sweet red peppers
2 large sweet green peppers
1/2 cup of salt
3 cups of cider vinegar
2 cups of brown sugar (tightly packed)
2 tablespoons of mixed whole pickling spices

Wash the tomatoes and cabbage. Peel the onions. Wash the peppers and remove seeds and membranes. Put all of the vegetables through a food chopper fitted with a medium blade, or chop them by hand. Put the chopped vegetables in a large glass bowl and sprinkle with the salt. Let stand in a cool place overnight. Rinse the vegetables under cold running water, draining them through a cheesecloth-lined sieve to remove all liquid. Combine the vinegar and sugar in a preserving kettle. Put the pickling spices in a cheesecloth bag and add to kettle. Bring to a boil, stirring, add the drained vegetables and simmer, uncovered, for 30 minutes. Remove spice bag and discard it. Ladle into hot, sterilized jars and seal immediately according to directions in Chapter 1. Process in a water bath 10 minutes.
Makes approximately 4 pints.

CHOW-CHOW

1 medium-size head of white cabbage
2 medium-size heads of cauliflower
4 medium-size tomatoes
1 large onion
4 medium-size sweet green peppers
2 medium-size sweet red peppers
3 tablespoons of salt
1-1/2 cups of sugar
2-1/2 cups of cider vinegar
2 teaspoons of dry mustard
1 teaspoon of turmeric
2 teaspoons of celery seeds
1 teaspoon of whole mustard seeds
1/2 teaspoon of ground ginger

Wash the cabbage, cauliflower and tomatoes. Peel the onion. Wash the peppers and remove seeds and membranes. Put all of the vegetables through a food chopper fitted with a medium blade, or chop them by hand. Put the chopped vegetables in a large glass bowl and sprinkle with the salt. Let stand in a cool place for about 6 hours. Rinse the vegetables under cold running water; drain well through a sieve. Combine the sugar, vinegar, dry mustard, turmeric, celery seeds, mustard seeds and ginger in a preserving kettle, bring to a boil, stirring, and simmer for 10 minutes. Add the drained vegetables and simmer, uncovered, for 10 minutes. Ladle into hot, sterilized jars and seal immediately according to directions in Chapter 1. Process in a water bath 10 minutes.
Makes approximately 4 pints.

CARROT RELISH

Tasty with cold chicken.

18 medium-size carrots
1 small cabbage
6 medium-size onions
1 large sweet red pepper
2 large sweet green peppers
2 cups of vinegar
3 cups of sugar (1-1/2 pounds)
1 tablespoon of whole mustard seeds
1 tablespoon of salt
1 tablespoon of celery seeds

Wash and peel the carrots. Wash and core the cabbage. Peel the onions. Wash the peppers and remove seeds and membranes. Put all of the vegetables through a food chopper fitted with a medium blade, or chop them by hand. Combine the vinegar, sugar, mustard seeds, salt and celery seeds in a preserving kettle. Add all of the vegetables, bring to a boil and simmer, uncovered, for 15 minutes. Ladle into hot, sterilized jars and seal immediately according to directions in Chapter 1. Process in a water bath 10 minutes.
Makes approximately 5 pints.

Pickles & Relishes

CUCUMBER RELISH

Complements cold poached salmon.

6 medium-size cucumbers
4 medium-size sweet green peppers
4 medium-size sweet red peppers
10 stalks of celery
1 large onion
1 tablespoon of turmeric
1/2 cup of salt
1-1/2 cups of brown sugar (tightly packed)
4 cups of vinegar
2 teaspoons of celery seeds
1 tablespoon of whole mustard seeds
2 teaspoons of whole cloves
2 teaspoons of whole allspice

Wash and peel the cucumbers. Wash the peppers and remove seeds and membranes. Wash the celery stalks. Peel the onion. Put all of the vegetables through a food chopper fitted with a medium blade, or chop them by hand. Put the chopped vegetables in a large glass bowl, sprinkle with turmeric and salt and add cold water to cover. Let stand in a cool place for about 4 hours. Drain the vegetables through a sieve and rinse under cold running water. Combine the sugar, vinegar, celery seeds and mustard seeds in a preserving kettle. Put the cloves and allspice in a cheesecloth bag, add to kettle and bring to a boil, stirring. Simmer for 5 minutes. Add the drained vegetables and simmer, uncovered, for 10 minutes. Remove the spice bag and discard it. Ladle into hot, sterilized jars and seal immediately according to directions in Chapter 1. Process in a water bath 10 minutes.
Makes approximately 6 pints.

CORN RELISH

A summer treat.

12 ears of sweet corn
2 pounds of onions
2 pounds of ripe tomatoes
2 pounds of cucumbers
3 sweet green peppers
3 sweet red peppers
1 head of celery
2 quarts of vinegar
6 small fresh or dried red chili peppers
1/4 cup of sugar
1/4 cup of salt
2 tablespoons of whole mustard seeds
2 tablespoons of turmeric

Drop ears of corn into boiling water and boil 5 minutes. Drain the corn and immerse in cold water. Cut the kernels from the cobs. Peel and chop the onions. Wash, blanch, peel and chop the tomatoes. Wash, peel and chop the cucumbers. Wash the sweet peppers, remove seeds and membranes and chop. Wash the celery, discard all but the heart and tender stalks and mince. Combine the vinegar, chili peppers, sugar, salt, mustard seeds and turmeric in a preserving kettle. Add all of the vegetables, bring to a boil and simmer, uncovered, for 1 hour. Ladle into hot, sterilized jars and seal immediately according to directions in Chapter 1. Process in a water bath 15 minutes.
Makes approximately 7 pints.

ZUCCHINI RELISH

Marvelous with hot dogs.

5 pounds of medium-size zucchini
6 large onions
1/2 cup of salt
2 cups of vinegar
1 cup of sugar
1 teaspoon of dry mustard
2 teaspoons of celery seeds
1/2 teaspoon of ground cinnamon
1/2 teaspoon of ground nutmeg
1/2 teaspoon of freshly ground black pepper
2 4-ounce jars of pimientos, drained

Wash the zucchini and cut off blossom and stem ends. Peel the onions. Put the zucchini and onions through a food chopper fitted with a medium blade, or chop by hand. Put the chopped vegetables in a large glass bowl, sprinkle with the salt and add cold water to cover. Cover with an inverted plate and place in the refrigerator overnight. The next morning, drain the vegetables through a sieve and rinse under cold running water. Combine the vinegar, sugar, dry mustard, celery seeds, cinnamon, nutmeg and pepper in a preserving kettle. Chop the pimientos and add to kettle with the drained vegetables. Bring to a boil, stirring occasionally, and simmer, uncovered, for 30 minutes. Ladle into hot, sterilized jars and seal immediately according to directions in Chapter 1. Process in a water bath 15 minutes.
Makes approximately 6 pints.

Pickles & Relishes

RIPE TOMATO RELISH

30 ripe tomatoes
24 sweet green peppers
18 medium-size onions
8-1/2 cups of cider vinegar
2 cups of sugar (1 pound)
3 tablespoons of salt
3 tablespoons of whole mustard seeds
1 tablespoon of ground allspice
1 tablespoon of ground mace
2 teaspoons of freshly ground black pepper
2 tablespoons of celery seeds

Wash the tomatoes. Wash the sweet peppers and remove seeds and membranes. Peel the onions. Put all of the vegetables through a food chopper fitted with a medium blade, or chop them by hand. Combine the vinegar, sugar, salt, mustard seeds, allspice, mace and ground pepper in a preserving kettle. Put the celery seeds in a cheesecloth bag and add to kettle with the chopped vegetables. Bring to a boil and simmer, uncovered, for about 3 hours until thick, stirring occasionally. Remove the spice bag and discard it. Ladle into hot, sterilized jars and seal immediately according to directions in Chapter 1. Process in a water bath 10 minutes.
Makes approximately 11 pints.

CHILI SAUCE

12 large ripe tomatoes
4 large sweet green peppers
1 large onion
2 cups of cider vinegar
1 cup of brown sugar (tightly packed)
1-1/2 teaspoons of ground allspice
1-1/2 teaspoons of salt
1-1/2 tablespoons of chili powder

Wash, blanch and peel the tomatoes. Wash the peppers and remove seeds and membranes. Peel the onion. Put all of the vegetables through a food chopper fitted with a medium blade, or chop them by hand. Combine the vinegar, sugar, allspice and salt in a preserving kettle. Add all of the vegetables, bring to a boil and simmer, uncovered, for 1-1/2 hours. Add the chili powder and simmer for 1-1/2 hours longer. Ladle into hot, sterilized jars and seal immediately according to directions in Chapter 1. Process in a water bath 15 minutes.
Makes approximately 2 pints.

TANGY TOMATO CATSUP

12 pounds of ripe tomatoes
3 medium-size onions
1 large sweet red pepper
1 tablespoon of whole mustard seeds
1 tablespoon of dried basil leaves
2 teaspoons of whole allspice
1 teaspoon of crushed, dried red chili pepper
1 large bay leaf
1 3-inch stick of cinnamon
1-1/2 cups of brown sugar (tightly packed)
1/4 teaspoon of ground ginger
1 tablespoon of salt
1 tablespoon of paprika
1 teaspoon of freshly ground black pepper
1 cup of cider vinegar

Wash and coarsely chop the tomatoes. Peel and coarsely chop the onions. Wash the sweet pepper, remove seeds and membranes and coarsely chop. Put the tomatoes, onions and sweet pepper in small amounts in a blender and blend until smooth. Now press the mixture through a wire sieve and discard the pulp. Put the purée into a preserving kettle and bring to a boil over medium heat. Simmer, uncovered, for 30 minutes. This should reduce the purée to about half the original volume. Put mustard seeds, basil, allspice, chili pepper, bay leaf and cinnamon in a cheesecloth bag and add to kettle. Add the brown sugar, ginger, salt, paprika and black pepper to the purée, stir well, and continue to simmer, uncovered, for 1-1/2 hours, stirring frequently to prevent sticking. Remove the spice bag and discard it. Add the vinegar to the kettle and simmer for 15 minutes. Ladle into hot, sterilized jars and seal immediately according to directions in Chapter 1. Process in a water bath 20 minutes.
Makes approximately 4 pints.

Pickles & Relishes

PICKLED HORSERADISH

A "must" with roast beef.

1 horseradish root
2 cups of vinegar
1 teaspoon of salt

Wash the horseradish root and peel with a vegetable peeler. Grate or mince the horseradish and pack into sterilized jars. Combine the vinegar and salt and pour over the horseradish to cover. Cover with an airtight cap and store in the refrigerator for 1 week before use. The horseradish will keep refrigerated for up to 6 weeks.
Makes approximately 2 half-pints.

PICKLED NASTURTIUM SEEDS

A poor man's caper.

Approximately 4 cups of green nasturtium
    seedpods
2 cups of wine vinegar
6 whole black peppercorns
1 tablespoon of salt

Pick the nasturtium seeds on a dry day. Wash and dry carefully, examining for insects. Peel and blanch the garlic clove. Combine the vinegar, peppercorns and salt in a 1-quart sterilized jar. Add enough nasturtium seeds to fill the bottle. Add the garlic and cover with an airtight cap. Store in the refrigerator for 3 to 4 weeks before use. The nasturtium seeds will keep refrigerated for up to 6 weeks.
Makes approximately 1 quart.

Bibliography

Apicius. *Roman Cookery: A Critical Translation of the Art of Cooking.* Tr. Barbara Flower and Elisabeth Rosenbaum. London: G.G. Harrap, 1958.

Appert, Nicolas. *The Art of Preserving All Kinds of Animal & Vegetable Substances for Several Years.* London: Black, Parry & Kingsbury, 1812.

Aresty, Esther B. *The Delectable Past.* New York: Simon & Schuster, 1964.

Ball, Edmund F. *From Fruit Jars to Satellites.* Muncie, Indiana: Ball Corporation, 1960.

Bax, Clifford. *Pretty Witty Nell.* London: Chapman & Hall, Ltd., 1932.

Beeton, Isabella M. *The Book of Household Management.* London: S.O. Beeton, 1861. New York: Farrar, Straus and Giroux, 1969.

Bitting, Katherine G. *Gastronomic Bibliography.* San Francisco: The Trade Pressroom, 1939.

Bitting, M.D., A.W. *Appertising.* San Francisco: The Trade Pressroom, 1937.

Boswell, James. *Life of Samuel Johnson.* London: Chatto & Windus, 1889.

Brillat-Savarin, J.A. *La Physiologie du Goût.* Tr. R.E. Anderson, M.A. London: Chatto & Windus, 1889.

Burbank, Luther, with Wilbur Hall. *Harvest of the Years.* Boston and New York: Houghton Mifflin Company, 1927.

Burbank, Luther. *Partner of Nature.* Edited by Wilbur Hall. New York and London: D. Appleton-Century Company, 1939.

Burke, John. *Duet in Diamonds.* New York: Putnam & Company, 1972.

Card, Fred W. *Bush Fruits.* New York: Macmillan & Company, 1925.

Cornaro, Luigi. *The Art of Living Long.* Milwaukee: W.F. Butler, 1903.

Dasent, A.I. *Nell Gwynne.* London: Macmillan & Company, 1924.

Dumas, A. *Dictionnaire de Cuisine.* Paris: A. Lemerre, Editeur, 1873.

Edwards, Everett D. *Washington, Jefferson, Lincoln and Agriculture.* Washington: U.S. Department of Agriculture, 1937.

Evelyn, John. *Aceteria.* Brooklyn: Brooklyn Botanical Garden, 1937.

Evelyn, John. *Diaries of John Evelyn.* London: Bickers and Son, 1879.

Fisher, M.F.K. *The Art of Eating.* New York: Macmillan & Company, 1954.

Fitzgibbon, Theodora. *A Taste of Scotland.* Boston: Houghton Mifflin Company, 1971.

Francatelli, C.A. *Francatelli's New Cook Book.* Philadelphia: D. McKay, 1895.

Glasse, Hannah. *The Art of Cookery.* London: By the Author, 1755.

Hazlitt, William C. *Old Cookery Books and Ancient Cuisine.* London: E. Stock, 1886.

Hearn, Lafcadio. *Creole Cuisine.* New Orleans: Hansell & Company, 1885.

Hearn, Lafcadio. *Creole Sketches.* Boston and New York: Houghton Mifflin Company, 1924.

Herbodeau, Eugene, and Paul Thalamas. *George Auguste Escoffier.* London: Practical Press, 1955.

Herman, Juliet, and Marguerite Herman. *Cornucopia.* New York: Harper & Row, 1973.

Hertzberg, Ruth, Beatrice Vaughan and Janet Greene. *Putting Food By.* Brattleboro, Vermont, 1973.

Hetherington, John. *Melba.* New York: Farrar, Straus and Giroux, 1968.

Hill, Janet M. *Canning, Preserving and Jelly Making.* Boston: Little, Brown & Company, 1915.

Hirtzler, Victor. *The Hotel St. Francis Cook Book.* Chicago: Hotel Monthly Press, 1919.

Bibliography

Holberg, Ruth. *Restless Johnny.* New York: Crowell Company, 1950.

Howe, Ruth. *Russian Cooking.* New York: Roy Inc., 1965.

Humelbergius Secundus (Dick). *Apician Morsels.* New York: J. & J. Harper, 1829.

Hyde, Montgomery. *Mr. & Mrs. Beeton.* London: G.G. Harrap, 1951.

Kerr Glass Manufacturing Company. *Kerr, Glass & You.* Sand Spring, Oklahoma, 1971.

Knight, Franklin (ed.). *Washington's Agricultural Correspondence.* Washington, D.C.: Published by the Editor, 1847.

Lincoln, Mrs. D.A. *Mrs. Lincoln's Boston Cook Book.* Boston: Roberts Bros., 1894.

McWilliams, V.S. *Lafcadio Hearn.* Boston: Houghton Mifflin Company, 1946.

Melba, Nellie. *Melodies and Memories.* London: T. Butterworth, Ltd., 1925.

Moody, Harriet C. *Mrs. William Vaughn Moody's Cookbook.* New York: Charles Scribner's Sons, 1931.

Morris, Lloyd. *Incredible New York.* New York: Bonanza Books, 1951.

Morris, T.N. *Principles of Food Preservation.* New York: Van Nostrand, 1938.

Neil, Marian H. *Canning, Pickling and Preserving.* New York: David McKay, 1914.

Oldham, Charles H. *The Cultivation of Berried Fruits in Great Britain.* London: C. Lockwood, 1946.

Pennell, E.R. *The Feasts of Autolycus.* London: John Lane, 1846.

Price, Robert. *Johnny Appleseed.* Bloomington: Indiana University Press, 1954.

Quennell, Nancy. *The Epicure's Anthology.* London: Golden Cockerel Press, 1936.

Rau, Santha Rama. *The Cooking of India.* New York: Time-Life Books, 1969.

Rector, George. *The Girls from Rector's.* Garden City: Doubleday & Company, 1927.

de la Reynière, A.B.G., and J.F. Coste. *Almanach des Gourmands.* Paris: J. Chaumerot, 1804-1812.

Rowland, Mabel. *Celebrated Actor Folk Cookery.* New York: Rowland, Inc., 1916.

Seely, L. *Mrs. Seely's Cook Book,* New York: Macmillan & Company, 1914.

Simmons, Amelia. *American Cookery.* New York: Hudson & Goodwin, 1796. Grand Rapids: Eerdmans, 1965.

Simmonds, P.L. *Tropical Agriculture.* London: E. & F. N. Spon, 1887.

Smith, Isabel C. *The Blue Book of Cookery.* New York: Funk & Wagnalls, 1926.

Soyer, Nicolas. *Soyer's Standard Cookery.* New York: Sturgis & Walton, 1912.

Spain, Nancy. *Mrs. Beeton and Her Husband.* London: Collins, 1948.

Toulouse, J.H. *The Men Behind the Fruit Jar.* Spinning Wheel, September, 1968.

Tschirsky, Oscar. *The Cookbook of 'Oscar' of the Waldorf.* Chicago and New York: Werener Company, 1896.

Varro, Marcus Terentius. *On Agriculture.* Tr. W.D. Hooper, M.A., Litt. D.; Loeb Classical Library. London: Wm. Heineman, 1934.

Vehling, J.D. *Apicius, De re coquinaria.* Cedar Rapids: Torch Press, 1936.

Vehling, J.D. *Platina and the Rebirth of Man.* Chicago: W.H. Hill, 1941.

Ward, Artemus. *The Encyclopedia of Food.* New York: Baker & Taylor Company, 1929.

Wilson, John H. *Nell Gwyn.* New York: Pellegrini & Cudahy, 1952.

Wolfe, Linda (ed.). *McCall's Introduction to British Cooking.* New York: Saturday Review Press, 1972.

Index

Index

Index

Biographical Notes

JACQUELINE WEJMAN learned the art of preserving as a girl in England during World War II when the English preserved all the food they could obtain. Since then she has been making preserves for Christmas gifts every year, using recipes of family and friends and creating her own variations. Among the appreciative recipients of these gifts were her former San Francisco neighbors, the late Charles St. Peter, a writer, and his wife, Genevieve. And thus the collaboration for the first edition of this book was born. Mrs. Wejman now lives in Sausalito.

CHARLES ST. PETER was a writer and newspaper editor with serious interest in food and history. A graduate of Georgetown University in Washington, D.C., he was city editor of the West Coast edition of the *Wall Street Journal,* a department editor of the *San Francisco Examiner* and city editor of *Pacific Stars and Stripes* in Tokyo. For several years before his death in 1978, he was a restaurant reviewer for the *California Critic* newsletter. In researching the essays for this book, he was assisted by his wife, Genevieve, a gourmet cook and one-time student at the Cordon Bleu in Paris.

HOLLY ZAPP has illustrated two other 101 Productions' cookbooks: *The Calculating Cook* and *More Calculated Cooking.* Mrs. Zapp has also animated several films for the "Sesame Street" television series. She and her husband Ivar, also an artist, divide their time between San Francisco and Costa Rica, where she teaches a course in book illustration.